FABRE'S BOOK OF INSECTS

*(retold from Alexander Teixeira de Mattos'
translation of Fabre's "Souvenirs Entomologiques"
by Mrs. Rodolph Stawell)*

Jean Henri Fabre

DOVER PUBLICATIONS, INC.
Mineola, New York

Published in Canada by General Publishing Company, Ltd., 30 Lesmill Road, Don Mills, Toronto, Ontario.

Published in the United Kingdom by Constable and Company, Ltd., 3 The Lanchesters, 162–164 Fulham Palace Road, London W6 9ER.

Bibliographical Note

This Dover edition, first published in 1998, is a republication of the work originally published by Dodd, Mead and Company, Inc., New York in 1921. While this book includes the unabridged text of the 1921 edition in its entirety, it does not contain the illustrations. A new Publisher's Note has been written for this edition.

Library of Congress Cataloging-in-Publication Data

Fabre, Jean-Henri, 1823–1915.
   [Souvenirs entomologiques. English]
   Fabre's book of insects (retold from Alexander Teixeira de Mattos' translation of Fabre's "Souvenirs entomologiques" by Mrs. Rodolph Stawell) / Jean Henri Fabre.
      p.   cm.
   Originally published: New York : Dodd, Mead and Co., 1921.
   ISBN 0-486-40152-9 (pbk.)
   1. Insects—Behavior.   I. Teixeira de Mattos, Alexander, 1865–1921.
II. Stawell, Rodolph, Mrs.   III. Title.
QL496.F13513   1998
595.7—dc21
                                          98-4171
                                          CIP

Manufactured in the United States of America
Dover Publications, Inc., 31 East 2nd Street, Mineola, N.Y. 11501

Contents

Contents

Publisher's Note

For more than 40 years—after his retirement from teaching—the French entomologist and belletrist, Jean Henri Fabre (1823–1915), devoted himself to studying the life history, habits, and instincts of insects through direct observation. His writings bring their mostly unobtrusive worlds alive with intricate detail and fascinating anecdote which enchant like a children's fairy tale, despite their thoroughly scientific grounding.

Dubbed "The Poet of Science" by one of his biographers, as well as the "Homer of Insects" by his contemporary, Charles Darwin, M. Fabre is almost forgotten today in his native France, and nearly unknown in the United States. But in Japan he is regarded as a pioneer in the science of ecology where his opus is widely read in new multi-volume translations. He is revered there too for his rather unique perspective on nature which directly links art and science.

Jean Henri Fabri's contemporary relevance is further enhanced by a recent British study on pheromones and insects which credits him with being the first to recognize the importance of smell in insect communication through his experiments with moths. Despite a potion of strong, noxious odors concocted to serve as an olfactory obstacle course, the male eggar moth was nonetheless able to detect the presence of the female solely from her scent.

Fabre's Book of Insects (from his *Souvenirs Entomologiques*) provides a fresh outlook on these creatures—on the wing and underfoot—with whom we share the earth.

CHAPTER I

My Work and My Workshop

We all have our own talents, our special gifts. Sometimes these gifts seem to come to us from our forefathers, but more often it is difficult to trace their origin.

A goatherd, perhaps, amuses himself by counting little pebbles and doing sums with them. He becomes an astoundingly quick reckoner, and in the end is a professor of mathematics. Another boy, at an age when most of us care only for play, leaves his schoolfellows at their games and listens to the imaginary sounds of an organ, a secret concert heard by him alone. He has a genius for music. A third—so small, perhaps, that he cannot eat his bread and jam without smearing his face—takes a keen delight in fashioning clay into little figures that are amazingly lifelike. If he be fortunate he will some day be a famous sculptor.

To talk about oneself is hateful, I know, but perhaps I may be allowed to do so for a moment, in order to introduce myself and my studies.

From my earliest childhood I have felt drawn towards the things of Nature. It would be ridiculous to suppose that this gift, this love of observing plants and insects, was inherited from my ancestors, who were uneducated people of the soil and observed little but their own cows and sheep. Of my four grandparents only one ever opened a book, and even he was very uncertain about his spelling. Nor do I owe anything to a scientific training. Without masters, without guides, often without books, I have gone forward with one aim always before me: to add a few pages to the history of insects.

As I look back—so many years back!—I can see myself as a tiny boy, extremely proud of my first braces and of my attempts to learn

1

the alphabet. And very well I remember the delight of finding my first bird's nest and gathering my first mushroom.

One day I was climbing a hill. At the top of it was a row of trees that had long interested me very much. From the little window at home I could see them against the sky, tossing before the wind or writhing madly in the snow, and I wished to have a closer view of them. It was a long climb—ever so long; and my legs were very short. I clambered up slowly and tediously, for the grassy slope was as steep as a roof.

Suddenly, at my feet, a lovely bird flew out from its hiding-place under a big stone. In a moment I had found the nest, which was made of hair and fine straw, and had six eggs laid side by side in it. The eggs were a magnificent azure blue, very bright. This was the first nest I ever found, the first of the many joys which the birds were to bring me. Overpowered with plea-sure, I lay down on the grass and stared at it.

Meanwhile the mother-bird was flying about uneasily from stone to stone, crying *"Tack! Tack!"* in a voice of the greatest anxiety. I was too small to understand what she was suffering. I made a plan worthy of a little beast of prey. I would carry away just one of the pretty blue eggs as a trophy, and then, in a fort-night, I would come back and take the tiny birds before they could fly away. Fortunately, as I walked carefully home, carrying my blue egg on a bed of moss, I met the priest.

"Ah!" said he. "A Saxicola's egg! Where did you get it?"

I told him the whole story. "I shall go back for the others," I said, "when the young birds have got their quill-feathers."

"Oh, but you mustn't do that!" cried the priest.

"You mustn't be so cruel as to rob the poor mother of all her little birds. Be a good boy, now, and promise not to touch the nest."

From this conversation I learnt two things: first, that robbing birds' nests is cruel and, secondly, that birds and beasts have names just like ourselves.

"What are the names of all my friends in the woods and meadows?" I asked myself. "And what does *Saxicola* mean?" Years later I learnt that *Saxicola* means an inhabitant of the rocks. My bird with the blue eggs was a Stone-chat.

Below our village there ran a little brook, and beyond the brook was a spinney of beeches with smooth, straight trunks, like pillars. The ground was padded with moss. It was in this spinney that I picked my first mushroom, which looked, when I caught sight of it, like an egg dropped on the moss by some wandering hen. There were many others there, of different sizes, forms, and colours. Some were shaped like bells, some like extinguishers, some like cups: some were broken, and were weeping tears of milk: some became blue when I trod on them. Others, the most curious of all, were like pears with a round hole at the top—a sort of chimney whence a whiff of smoke escaped when I prodded their under-side with my finger. I filled my pockets with these, and made them smoke at my leisure, till at last they were reduced to a kind of tinder.

Many a time I returned to that delightful spinney, and learnt my first lessons in mushroom-lore in the company of the Crows. My collections, I need hardly say, were not admitted to the house.

In this way—by observing Nature and making experiments—nearly all my lessons have been learnt: all except two, in fact. I have received from others two lessons of a scientific character, and two only, in the whole course of my life: one in anatomy and one in chemistry.

I owe the first to the learned naturalist Moquin-Tandon, who showed me how to explore the interior of a Snail in a plate filled with water. The lesson was short and fruitful.[1]

My first introduction to chemistry was less fortunate. It ended in the bursting of a glass vessel, with the result that most of my fellow-pupils were hurt, one of them nearly lost his sight, the lecturer's clothes were burnt to pieces, and the wall of the lecture-room was splashed with stains. Later on, when I returned to that room, no longer as a pupil but as a master, the splashes were still there. On that occasion I learnt one thing at least. Ever after, when I made experiments of that kind, I kept my pupils at a distance.

---

[1] See Insect Adventures, retold for young people from the works of Henri Fabre.

It has always been my great desire to have a laboratory in the open fields—not an easy thing to obtain when one lives in a state of constant anxiety about one's daily bread. For forty years it was my dream to own a little bit of land, fenced in for the sake of privacy: a desolate, barren, sun-scorched bit of land, overgrown with thistles and much beloved by Wasps and Bees. Here, without fear of interruption, I might question the Hunting-wasps and others of my friends in that difficult language which consists of experiments and observations. Here, without the long expeditions and rambles that use up my time and strength, I might watch my insects at every hour of the day.

And then, at last, my wish was fulfilled. I obtained a bit of land in the solitude of a little village. It was a *harmas,* which is the name we give in this part of Provence to an untilled, pebbly expanse where hardly any plant but thyme can grow. It is too poor to be worth the trouble of ploughing, but the sheep pass there in spring, when it has chanced to rain and a little grass grows up.

My own particular *harmas,* however, had a small quantity of red earth mixed with the stones, and had been roughly cultivated. I was told that vines once grew here, and I was sorry, for the original vegetation had been driven out by the three-pronged fork. There was no thyme left, nor lavender, nor a single clump of the dwarf oak. As thyme and lavender might be useful to me as a hunting-ground for Bees and Wasps, I was obliged to plant them again.

There were plenty of weeds: couch-grass, and prickly centauries, and the fierce Spanish oyster-plant, with its spreading orange flowers and spikes strong as nails. Above it towered the Illyrian cotton-thistle, whose straight and solitary stalk grows sometimes to the height of six feet and ends in large pink tufts. There were smaller thistles too, so well armed that the plant-collector can hardly tell where to grasp them, and spiky knapweeds, and in among them, in long lines provided with hooks, the shoots of the blue dewberry creeping along the ground. If you had visited this prickly thicket without wearing high boots, you would have paid dearly for your rashness!

Such was the Eden that I won by forty years of desperate struggle.

This curious, barren Paradise of mine is the happy hunting-ground of countless Bees and Wasps. Never have I seen so large a population of insects at a single spot. All the trades have made it their centre. Here come hunters of every kind of game, builders in clay, cotton-weavers, leaf-cutters, architects in paste-board, plasterers mixing mortar, carpenters boring wood, miners digging underground galleries, workers in gold-beaters' skin, and many more.

See—here is a Tailor-bee. She scrapes the cobwebby stalk of the yellow-flowered centaury, and gathers a ball of wadding which she carries off proudly with her mandibles or jaws. She will turn it, underground, into cotton satchels to hold the store of honey and the eggs. And here are the Leaf-cutting Bees, carrying their black, white, or blood-red reaping brushes under their bodies. They will visit the neighbouring shrubs, and there cut from the leaves oval pieces in which to wrap their harvest. Here too are the black, velvet-clad Mason-bees, who work with cement and gravel. We could easily find specimens of their masonry on the stones in the *harmas.* Next comes a kind of Wild Bee who stacks her cells in the winding staircase of an empty snail-shell; and another who lodges her grubs in the pith of a dry bramble-stalk; and a third who uses the channel of a cut reed; and a fourth who lives rent-free in the vacant galleries of some Mason-bee. There are also Bees with horns, and Bees with brushes on their hind-legs, to be used for reaping.

While the walls of my *harmas* were being built some great heaps of stones and mounds of sand were scattered here and there by the builders, and were soon occupied by a variety of inhabitants. The Mason-bees chose the chinks between the stones for their sleeping-place. The powerful Eyed Lizard, who, when hard pressed, attacks both man and dog, selected a cave in which to lie in wait for the passing Scarab, or Sacred Beetle. The Black-eared Chat, who looks like a Dominican monk in his white-and-black raiment, sat on the top stone singing his brief song. His nest, with the sky-blue eggs, must have been somewhere in the heap. When the stones were moved the little

Dominican moved too. I regret him: he would have been a charming neighbour. The Eyed Lizard I do not regret at all.

The sand-heaps sheltered a colony of Digger-wasps and Hunting-wasps, who were, to my sorrow, turned out at last by the builders. But still there are hunters left: some who flutter about in search of Caterpillars, and one very large kind of Wasp who actually has the courage to hunt the Tarantula. Many of these mighty Spiders have their burrows in the *harmas*, and you can see their eyes gleaming at the bottom of the den like little diamonds. On hot summer afternoons you may also see Amazon-ants, who leave their barracks in long battalions and march far afield to hunt for slaves.

Nor are these all. The shrubs about the house are full of birds, Warblers and Greenfinches, Sparrows and Owls; while the pond is so popular with the Frogs that in May it becomes a deafening orchestra. And boldest of all, the Wasp has taken possession of the house itself. On my doorway lives the White-banded Sphex: when I go indoors I must be careful not to tread upon her as she carries on her work of mining. Just within a closed window a kind of Mason-wasp has made her earth-built nest upon the freestone wall. To enter her home she uses a little hole left by accident in the shutters. On the mouldings of the Venetian blinds a few stray Mason-bees build their cells. The Common Wasp and the Solitary Wasp visit me at dinner. The object of their visit, apparently, is to see if my grapes are ripe.

Such are my companions. My dear beasts, my friends of former days and other more recent acquaintances, are all here, hunting, and building, and feeding their families. And if I wish for change the mountain is close to me, with its tangle of arbutus, and rock-roses, and heather, where Wasps and Bees delight to gather. And that is why I deserted the town for the village, and came to Sérignan to weed my turnips and water my lettuces.

CHAPTER II

The Sacred Beetle

I

The Ball

It is six or seven thousand years since the Sacred Beetle was first talked about. The peasant of ancient Egypt, as he watered his patch of onions in the spring, would see from time to time a fat black insect pass close by, hurriedly trundling a ball backwards. He would watch the queer rolling thing in amazement, as the peasant of Provence watches it to this day.

The early Egyptians fancied that this ball was a symbol of the earth, and that all the Scarab's actions were prompted by the movements of the heavenly bodies. So much knowledge of astronomy in a Beetle seemed to them almost divine, and that is why he is called the Sacred Beetle. They also thought that the ball he rolled on the ground contained the egg, and that the young Beetle came out of it. But as a matter of fact, it is simply his store of food.

It is not at all nice food. For the work of this Beetle is to scour the filth from the surface of the soil. The ball he rolls so carefully is made of his sweepings from the roads and fields.

This is how he sets about it. The edge of his broad, flat head is notched with six teeth arranged in a semi-circle, like a sort of curved rake; and this he uses for digging and cutting up, for throwing aside the stuff he does not want, and scraping together the food he chooses. His bow-shaped fore-legs are also useful tools, for they are very strong, and they too have five teeth on the outside. So if a vigorous effort be needed to remove some obstacle the Scarab makes use of his elbows, that is to say he flings his toothed legs to right and left, and clears a space with an energetic sweep. Then he collects armfuls of the stuff he has

7

raked together, and pushes it beneath him, between the four hinder-legs. These are long and slender, especially the last pair, slightly bowed and finished with a sharp claw. The Beetle then presses the stuff against his body with his hind-legs, curving it and spinning it round and round till it forms a perfect ball. In a moment a tiny pellet grows to the size of a walnut, and soon to that of an apple. I have seen some gluttons manufacture a ball as big as a man's fist.

When the ball of provisions is ready it must be moved to a suitable place. The Beetle begins the journey. He clasps the ball with his long hind-legs and walks with his fore-legs, moving backwards with his head down and his hind-quarters in the air. He pushes his load behind him by alternate thrusts to right and left. One would expect him to choose a level road, or at least a gentle incline. Not at all! Let him find himself near some steep slope, impossible to climb, and that is the very path the obstinate creature will attempt. The ball, that enormous burden, is painfully hoisted step by step, with infinite precautions, to a certain height, always backwards. Then by some rash movement all this toil is wasted: the ball rolls down, dragging the Beetle with it. Once more the heights are climbed, and another fall is the result. Again and again the insect begins the ascent. The merest trifle ruins everything; a grass-root may trip him up or a smooth bit of gravel make him slip, and down come ball and Beetle, all mixed up together. Ten or twenty times he will start afresh, till at last he is successful, or else sees the hopelessness of his efforts and resigns himself to taking the level road.

Sometimes the Scarab seems to enter into partnership with a friend. This is the way in which it usually happens. When the Beetle's ball is ready he leaves the crowd of workers, pushing his prize backwards. A neighbour, whose own task is hardly begun, suddenly drops his work and runs to the moving ball, to lend a hand to the owner. His aid seems to be accepted willingly. But the new-comer is not really a partner: he is a robber. To make one's own ball needs hard work and patience; to steal one ready-made, or to invite oneself to a neighbour's dinner, is much easier. Some thieving Beetles go to work craftily, others use violence.

Sometimes a thief comes flying up, knocks over the owner of the ball, and perches himself on top of it. With his fore-legs crossed over his breast, ready to hit out, he awaits events. If the owner raises himself to seize his ball the robber gives him a blow that stretches him on his back. Then the owner gets up and shakes the ball till it begins rolling, and perhaps the thief falls off. A wrestling-match follows. The two Beetles grapple with one another: their legs lock and unlock, their joints intertwine, their horny armour clashes and grates with the rasping sound of metal under a file. The one who is successful climbs to the top of the ball, and after two or three attempts to dislodge him the defeated Scarab goes off to make himself a new pellet. I have sometimes seen a third Beetle appear, and rob the robber.

But sometimes the thief bides his time and trusts to cunning. He pretends to help the victim to roll the food along, over sandy plains thick with thyme, over cart-ruts and steep places, but he really does very little of the work, preferring to sit on the ball and do nothing. When a suitable place for a burrow is reached the rightful owner begins to dig with his sharp-edged forehead and toothed legs, flinging armfuls of sand behind him, while the thief clings to the ball, shamming dead. The cave grows deeper and deeper, and the working Scarab disappears from view. Whenever he comes to the surface he glances at the ball, on which the other lies, demure and motionless, inspiring confidence. But as the absences of the owner become longer the thief seizes his chance, and hurriedly makes off with the ball, which he pushes behind him with the speed of a pickpocket afraid of being caught. If the owner catches him, as sometimes happens, he quickly changes his position, and seems to plead as an excuse that the pellet rolled down the slope, and he was only trying to stop it! And the two bring the ball back as though nothing had happened.

If the thief has managed to get safely away, however, the owner can only resign himself to his loss, which he does with admirable fortitude. He rubs his cheeks, sniffs the air, flies off, and begins his work all over again. I admire and envy his character.

At last his provisions are safely stored. His burrow is a shallow hole about the size of a man's fist, dug in soft earth or sand, with a short passage to the surface, just wide enough to admit the ball. As soon as his food is rolled into this burrow the Scarab shuts himself in by stopping up the entrance with rubbish. The ball fills almost the whole room: the banquet rises from floor to ceiling. Only a narrow passage runs between it and the walls, and here sit the banqueters, two at most, very often only one. Here the Sacred Beetle feasts day and night, for a week or a fortnight at a time, without ceasing.

II

The Pear

As I have already said, the ancient Egyptians thought that the egg of the Sacred Beetle was within the ball that I have been describing. I have proved that it is not so. One day I discovered the truth about the Scarab's egg.

A young shepherd who helps me in his spare time came to me one Sunday in June with a queer thing in his hand. It was exactly like a tiny pear that had lost all its fresh colour and had turned brown in rotting. It was firm to the touch and very graceful in shape, though the materials of which it was formed seemed none too nicely chosen. The shepherd assured me there was an egg inside it; for a similar pear, crushed by accident in the digging, had contained a white egg the size of a grain of wheat.

At daybreak the next morning the shepherd and I went out to investigate the matter. We met among the browsing sheep, on some slopes that had lately been cleared of trees.

A Sacred Beetle's burrow is soon found: you can tell it by the fresh little mound of earth above it. My companion dug vigorously into the ground with my pocket trowel, while I lay down, the better to see what was being unearthed. A cave opened out, and there I saw, lying in the moist earth, a splendid pear upon the ground. I shall not soon forget my first sight of the mother Beetle's wonderful work. My excitement could have been no greater had I, in digging among the relics of ancient Egypt, found the sacred insect carved in emerald.

We went on with our search, and found a second hole. Here,

by the side of the pear and fondly embracing it, was the mother Beetle, engaged no doubt in giving it the finishing touches before leaving the burrow for good. There was no possible doubt that the pear was the nest of the Scarab. In the course of the summer I found at least a hundred such nests.

The pear, like the ball, is formed of refuse scraped up in the fields, but the materials are less coarse, because they are intended for the food of the grub. When it comes out of the egg it is incapable of searching for its own meals, so the mother arranges that it shall find itself surrounded by the food that suits it best. It can begin eating at once, without further trouble.

The egg is laid in the narrow end of the pear. Every germ of life, whether of plant or animal, needs air: even the shell of a bird's egg is riddled with an endless number of pores. If the germ of the Scarab were in the thick part of the pear it would be smothered, because there the materials are very closely packed, and are covered with a hard rind. So the mother Beetle prepares a nice airy room with thin walls for her little grub to live in, during its first moments. There is a certain amount of air even in the very centre of the pear, but not enough for a delicate baby-grub. By the time he has eaten his way to the centre he is strong enough to manage with very little air.

There is, of course, a good reason for the hardness of the shell that covers the big end of the pear. The Scarab's burrow is extremely hot: sometimes the temperature reaches boiling point. The provisions, even though they have to last only three or four weeks, are liable to dry up and become uneatable. When, instead of the soft food of its first meal, the unhappy grub finds nothing to eat but horrible crusty stuff as hard as a pebble, it is bound to die of hunger. I have found numbers of these victims of the August sun. The poor things are baked in a sort of closed oven. To lessen this danger the mother Beetle compresses the outer layer of the pear—or nest—with all the strength of her stout, flat forearms, to turn it into a protecting rind like the shell of a nut. This helps to ward off the heat. In the hot summer months the housewife puts her bread into a closed pan to keep it fresh. The insect does the same in its own fashion: by dint of pressure it covers the family bread with a pan.

I have watched the Sacred Beetle at work in her den, so I know how she makes her pear-shaped nest.

With the building-materials she has collected she shuts herself up underground so as to give her whole attention to the business in hand. The materials may be obtained in two ways. As a rule, under natural conditions, she kneads a ball in the usual way and rolls it to a favourable spot. As it rolls along it hardens a little on the surface and gathers a slight crust of earth and tiny grains of sand, which is useful later on. Now and then, however, the Beetle finds a suitable place for her burrow quite close to the spot where she collects her building-materials, and in that case she simply bundles armfuls of stuff into the hole. The result is most striking. One day I see a shapeless lump disappear into the burrow. Next day, or the day after, I visit the Beetle's workshop and find the artist in front of her work. The formless mass of scrapings has become a pear, perfect in outline and exquisitely finished.

The part that rests on the floor of the burrow is crusted over with particles of sand, while the rest is polished like glass. This shows that the Beetle has not rolled the pear round and round, but has shaped it where it lies. She has modelled it with little taps of her broad feet, just as she models her ball in the daylight.

By making an artificial burrow for the mother Beetle in my own workshop, with the help of a glass jar full of earth, and a peep-hole through which I can observe operations, I have been able to see the work in its various stages.

The Beetle first makes a complete ball. Then she starts the neck of the pear by making a ring round the ball and applying pressure, till the ring becomes a groove. In this way a blunt projection is pushed out at one side of the ball. In the centre of this projection she employs further pressure to form a sort of crater or hollow, with a swollen rim; and gradually the hollow is made deeper and the swollen rim thinner and thinner, till a sack is formed. In this sack, which is polished and glazed inside, the egg is laid. The opening of the sack, or extreme end of the pear, is then closed with a plug of stringy fibres.

There is a reason for this rough plug—a most curious exception, when nothing else has escaped the heavy blows of the insect's leg. The end of the egg rests against it, and, if the stopper were pressed down and driven in, the infant grub might suffer. So the Beetle stops the hole without ramming down the stopper.

III

The Growing-Up of the Scarab

About a week or ten days after the laying of the egg, the grub is hatched, and without delay begins to eat its house. It is a grub of remarkable wisdom, for it always starts its meal with the thickest part of the walls, and so avoids making a hole through which it might fall out of the pear altogether. It soon becomes fat; and indeed it is an ungainly creature at best, with an enormous hump on its back, and a skin so transparent that if you hold it up to the light you can see its internal organs. If the early Egyptian had chanced upon this plump white grub he would never have suspected it to contain, in an undeveloped state, the sober beauty of the Scarab!

When first it sheds its skin the insect that appears is not a full-grown Scarab, though all the Scarab's features can be recognised. There are few insects so beautiful as this delicate creature with its wing-cases lying in front of it like a wide pleated scarf and its forelegs folded under its head. Half transparent and as yellow as honey, it looks as though it were carved from a block of amber. For four weeks it remains in this state, and then it too casts its skin.

Its colouring now is red-and-white,—so many times does the Sacred Beetle change its garments before it finally appears black as ebony! As it grows blacker it also grows harder, till it is covered with horny armour and is a full-grown Beetle.

All this time he is underground, in the pear-shaped nest. Great is his longing to burst the shell of his prison and come into the sunshine. Whether he succeeds in doing so depends on circumstances.

It is generally August when he is ready for release, and August as a rule is the driest and hottest month of the year. If therefore no rain falls to soften the earth, the cell to be burst and the wall to be broken defy the strength of the insect, which is helpless against all that hardness. The soft material of the nest has become an impassable rampart; it has turned into a sort of brick, baked in the kiln of summer.

I have, of course, made experiments on insects that are ready to be released. I lay the hard, dry shells in a box where they remain dry; and sooner or later I hear a sharp, grating sound inside each cell. It is the prisoner scraping the wall with the rakes on his forehead and his fore-feet. Two or three days pass, and no progress seems to have been made.

I try to help a couple of them by opening a loophole with my knife; but these favoured ones make no more progress than the others.

In less than a fortnight silence reigns in all the shells. The prisoners, worn out with their efforts, have all died.

Then I take some other shells, as hard as the first, wrap them in a wet rag, and put them in a corked flask. When the moisture has soaked through them I rid them of the wrapper, but keep them in the flask. This time the experiment is a complete success. Softened by the wet the shells are burst by the prisoner, who props himself boldly on his legs, using his back as a lever, or else scrapes away at one point till the walls crumble to pieces. In every case the Beetle is released.

In natural conditions, when the shells remain underground, the same thing occurs. When the soil is burnt by the August sun it is impossible for the insect to wear away his prison, which is hard as a brick. But when a shower comes the shell recovers the softness of its early days: the insect struggles with his legs and pushes with his back, and so becomes free.

At first he shows no interest in food. What he wants above all is the joy of the light. He sets himself in the sun, and there, motionless, basks in the warmth.

Presently, however, he wishes to eat. With no one to teach him, he sets to work, exactly like his elders, to make himself a ball of food. He digs his burrow and stores it with provisions. Without ever learning it, he knows his trade to perfection.

CHAPTER III

The Cicada

I

The Cicada and the Ant

To most of us the Cicada's song is unknown, for he lives in the land of the olive-trees. But every one who has read La Fontaine's "Fables" has heard of the snub the Cicada received from the Ant, though La Fontaine was not the first to tell the tale.

The Cicada, says the story, did nothing but sing all through the summer, while the Ants were busy storing their provisions. When winter came he was hungry, and hurried to his neighbour to borrow some food. He met with a poor welcome.

"Why didn't you gather your food in the summer?" asked the prudent Ant.

"I was busy singing all the summer," said the Cicada.

"Singing, were you?" answered the Ant unkindly. "Well, then, now you may dance!" And she turned her back on the beggar.

Now the insect in this fable could not possibly be a Cicada. La Fontaine, it is plain, was thinking of the Grasshopper and as a matter of fact the English translations usually substitute a Grasshopper for the Cicada.

For my village does not contain a peasant so ignorant as to imagine the Cicada ever exists in winter. Every tiller of the soil is familiar with the grub of this insect, which he turns over with his spade whenever he banks up the olive-trees at the approach of cold weather. A thousand times he has seen the grub leave the ground through a round hole of its own making, fasten itself to a twig, split its own back, take off its skin, and turn into a Cicada.

The fable is a slander. The Cicada is no beggar, though it is

15

true that he demands a good deal of attention from his neighbours. Every summer he comes and settles in his hundreds outside my door, amid the greenery of two tall plane-trees; and here, from sunrise to sunset, he tortures my head with the rasping of his harsh music. This deafening concert, this incessant rattling and drumming, makes all thought impossible.

It is true, too, that there are sometimes dealings between the Cicada and the Ant; but they are exactly the opposite of those described in the fable. The Cicada is never dependent on others for his living. At no time does he go crying famine at the doors of the Ant-hills. On the contrary, it is the Ant who, driven by hunger, begs and entreats the singer. Entreats, did I say? It is not the right word. She brazenly robs him.

In July, when most of the insects in my sunny country are parched with thirst, and vainly wander round the withered flowers in search of refreshment, the Cicada remains perfectly cheerful. With his rostrum—the delicate sucker, sharp as a gimlet, that he carries on his chest—he broaches a cask in his inexhaustible cellar. Sitting, always singing, on the branch of a shrub, he bores through the firm, smooth bark, which is swollen with sap. Driving his sucker through the bunghole, he drinks his fill.

If I watch him for a little while I may perhaps see him in unexpected trouble. There are many thirsty insects in the neighbourhood, who soon discover the sap that oozes from the Cicada's well. They hasten up, at first quietly and discreetly, to lick the fluid as it comes out. I see Wasps, Flies, Earwigs, Rose-chafers, and above all, Ants.

The smallest, in order to reach the well, slip under the body of the Cicada, who good-naturedly raises himself on his legs to let them pass. The larger insects snatch a sip, retreat, take a walk on a neighbouring branch, and then return more eager and enterprising than before. They now become violent brigands, determined to chase the Cicada away from his well.

The worst offenders are the Ants. I have seen them nibbling at the ends of the Cicada's legs, tugging at the tips of his wings, and climbing on his back. Once a bold robber, before my very eyes, caught hold of a Cicada's sucker and tried to pull it out.

At last, worried beyond all patience, the singer deserts the well he has made. The Ant has now attained her object: she is left in possession of the spring. This dries up very soon, it is true; but, having drunk all the sap that is there, she can wait for another drink till she has a chance of stealing another well.

So you see that the actual facts are just the reverse of those in the fable. The Ant is the hardened beggar: the industrious worker is the Cicada.

II

The Cicada's Burrow

I am in an excellent position to study the habits of the Cicada, for I live in his company. When July comes he takes possession of the enclosures right up to the threshold of the house. I remain master indoors, but out of doors he reigns supreme, and his reign is by no means a peaceful one.

The first Cicadæ appear at midsummer. In the much-trodden, sun-baked paths I see, level with the ground, round holes about the size of a man's thumb. Through these holes the Cicada-grubs come up from the underground to be transformed into full-grown Cicadæ on the surface. Their favourite places are the driest and sunniest; for these grubs are provided with such powerful tools that they can bore through baked earth or sandstone. When I examine their deserted burrows I have to use my pickaxe.

The first thing one notices is that the holes, which measure nearly an inch across, have absolutely no rubbish round them. There is no mound of earth thrown up outside. Most of the digging insects, such as the Dorbeetles for instance, make a mole-hill above their burrows. The reason for this difference lies in their manner of working. The Dorbeetle begins his work at the mouth of the hole, so he can heap up on the surface the material he digs out: but the Cicada-grub comes up from below. The last thing he does is to make the doorway, and he cannot heap rubbish on a threshold that does not yet exist.

The Cicada's tunnel runs to a depth of fifteen or sixteen inches. It is quite open the whole way. It ends in a rather wider space, but is completely closed at the bottom. What has become of the earth removed to make this tunnel? And why do not the walls crumble? One would expect that the grub, climbing up and down with his clawed legs, would make landslips and block up his own house.

Well, he behaves like a miner or a railway-engineer. The miner holds up his galleries with pit-props; the builder of railways strengthens his tunnel with a casing of brickwork; the Cicada is as clever as either of them, and covers the walls of his tunnel with cement. He carries a store of sticky fluid hidden within him, with which to make this plaster. His burrow is always built above some tiny rootlet containing sap, and from this root he renews his supply of fluid.

It is very important for him to be able to run up and down his burrow at his ease, because, when the time comes for him to find his way into the sunshine, he wants to know what the weather is like outside. So he works away for weeks, perhaps for months, to make a funnel with good strong plastered walls, on which he can clamber. At the top he leaves a layer as thick as one's finger, to protect him from the outer air till the last moment. At the least hint of fine weather he scrambles up, and, through the thin lid at the top, inquires into the state of the weather.

If he suspects a storm or rain on the surface—matter of great importance to a delicate grub when he takes off his skin!—he slips prudently back to the bottom of his snug funnel. But if the weather seems warm he smashes his ceiling with a few strokes of his claws, and climbs to the surface.

It is the fluid substance carried by the Cicada-grub in his swollen body that enables him to get rid of the rubbish in his burrow. As he digs he sprinkles the dusty earth and turns it into paste. The walls then become soft and yielding. The mud squeezes into the chinks of the rough soil, and the grub compresses it with his fat body. This is why, when he appears at the top, he is always covered with wet stains.

For some time after the Cicada-grub's first appearance above-ground he wanders about the neighbourhood, looking for a suitable spot in which to cast off his skin—a tiny bush, a tuft of thyme, a blade of grass, or the twig of a shrub. When he finds it he climbs up, and clings to it firmly with the claws of his fore-feet. His fore-legs stiffen into an immovable grip.

Then his outer skin begins to split along the middle of the back, showing the pale-green Cicada within. Presently the head is free; then the sucker and front legs appear, and finally the hind-legs and the rumpled wings. The whole insect is free now, except the extreme tip of his body.

He next performs a wonderful gymnastic feat. High in the air as he is, fixed to his old skin at one point only, he turns himself over till his head is hanging downwards. His crumpled wings straighten out, unfurl, and spread themselves. Then with an almost invisible movement he draws himself up again by sheer strength, and hooks his fore-legs on to his empty skin. This movement has released the tip of his body from its sheath. The whole operation has taken about half an hour.

For a time the freed Cicada does not feel very strong. He must bathe in air and sunshine before strength and colour come to his frail body. Hanging to his cast skin by his fore-claws only, he sways at the least breath of air, still feeble and still green. But at last the brown tinge appears, and is soon general. Supposing him to have taken possession of the twig at nine o'clock in the morning, the Cicada flies away at half-past twelve, leaving his cast skin behind him. Sometimes it hangs from the twigs for months.

III

The Cicada's Music

The Cicada, it appears, loves singing for its own sake. Not content with carrying an instrument called the cymbal in a cavity behind his wings, he increases its power by means of sounding-boards under his chest. Indeed, there is one kind of Cicada who sacrifices a great deal in order to give full play to his musical tastes. He carries such an enormous sounding-board that there is hardly any room left for his vital organs, which are squeezed into a tiny corner. Assuredly one must be passionately devoted to music thus to clear away one's internal organs in order to make room for a musical box!

Unfortunately the song he loves so much is extremely unattractive to others. Nor have I yet discovered its object. It is usually suggested that he is calling his mate; but the facts appear to contradict this idea.

For fifteen years the Common Cicada has thrust his society upon me. Every summer for two months I have these insects before my eyes, and their song in my ears. I see them ranged in rows on the smooth bark of the plane-trees, the maker of music and his mate sitting side by side. With their suckers driven into the tree they drink, motionless. As the sun turns they also turn round the branch with slow, sidelong steps, to find the hottest spot. Whether drinking or moving they never cease singing.

It seems unlikely, therefore, that they are calling their mates. You do not spend months on end calling to some one who is at your elbow.

Indeed, I am inclined to think that the Cicada himself cannot even hear the song he sings with so much apparent delight. This might account for the relentless way in which he forces his music upon others.

He has very clear sight. His five eyes tell him what is happening to right and to left and above his head; and the moment he sees any one coming he is silent and flies away. Yet no noise disturbs him. Place yourself behind him, and then talk, whistle, clap your hands, and knock two stones together. For much less than this a bird, though he would not see you, would fly away terrified. The imperturbable Cicada goes on rattling as though nothing were there.

On one occasion I borrowed the local artillery, that is to say the guns that are fired on feast-days in the village. There were two of them, and they were crammed with powder as though for the most important rejoicings. They were placed at the foot of the plane-trees in front of my door. We were careful to leave the windows open, to prevent the panes from breaking. The Cicadæ in the branches overhead could not see what was happening.

Six of us waited below, eager to hear what would be the effect on the orchestra above.

Bang! The gun went off with a noise like a thunderclap.

Quite unconcerned, the Cicadæ continued to sing. Not one appeared in the least disturbed. There was no change whatever in the quality or the quantity of the sound. The second gun had no more effect than the first.

I think, after this experiment, we must admit that the Cicada is hard of hearing, and like a very deaf man, is quite unconscious that he is making a noise.

IV

The Cicada's Eggs

The Common Cicada likes to lay her eggs on small dry branches. She chooses, as far as possible, tiny stalks, which may be of any size between that of a straw and a lead-pencil. The sprig is never lying on the ground, is usually nearly upright in position, and is almost always dead.

Having found a twig to suit her, she makes a row of pricks with the sharp instrument on her chest—such pricks as might be made with a pink if it were driven downwards on a slant, so as to tear the fibres and force them slightly upwards. If she is undisturbed she will make thirty or forty of these pricks on the same twig.

In the tiny cells formed by these pricks she lays her eggs. The cells are narrow passages, each one slanting down towards the one below it. I generally find about ten eggs in each cell, so it is plain that the Cicada lays between three and four hundred eggs altogether.

This is a fine family for one insect. The numbers point to some special danger that threatens the Cicada, and makes it necessary to produce a great quantity of grubs lest some should be destroyed. After many observations I have discovered what this danger is. It is an extremely tiny Gnat, compared with which the Cicada is a monster.

This Gnat, like the Cicada, carries a boring-tool. It is planted beneath her body, near the middle, and sticks out at right angles. As fast as the Cicada lays her eggs the Gnat tries to destroy them. It is a real scourge to the Cicada family. It is amazing to watch her calm and brazen audacity in the presence of the giant who could crush her by simply stepping on her. I have seen as many as three preparing to despoil one unhappy Cicada at the same time, standing close behind one another.

The Cicada has just stocked a cell with eggs, and is climbing a little higher to make another cell. One of the brigands runs to the spot she has just left; and here, almost under the claws of the monster, as calmly and fearlessly as though she were at home, the Gnat bores a second hole above the Cicada's eggs, and places among them an egg of her own. By the time the Cicada flies away most of her cells have, in this way, received a stranger's egg, which will be the ruin of hers. A small quick-hatching grub, one only to each cell, handsomely fed on a dozen raw eggs, will take the place of the Cicada's family.

This deplorable mother has learnt nothing from centuries of experience. Her large and excellent eyes cannot fail to see the terrible felons fluttering round her. She must know they are at her heels, and yet she remains unmoved, and lets herself be victimised. She could easily crush the wicked atoms, but she is incapable of altering her instincts, even to save her family from destruction.

Through my magnifying-glass I have seen the hatching of the Cicada's eggs. When the grub first appears it has a marked likeness to an extremely small fish, with large black eyes, and a curious sort of mock fin under its body, formed of the two fore-legs joined together. This fin has some power of movement, and helps the grub to work its way out of the shell, and also—a much more difficult matter—out of the fibrous stem in which it is imprisoned.

As soon as this fish-like object has made its way out of the cell it sheds its skin. But the cast skin forms itself into a thread, by which the grub remains fastened to the twig or stem. Here, before dropping to the ground, it treats itself to a sun-bath, kicking about and trying its strength, or swinging lazily at the end of its rope.

Its antennæ now are free, and wave about; its legs work their joints; those in front open and shut their claws. I know hardly any more curious sight than this tiny acrobat hanging by the tip of its body, swinging at the least breath of wind, and making ready in the air for its somersault into the world.

Sooner or later, without losing much time, it drops to the ground. The little creature, no bigger than a Flea, has saved its tender body from the rough earth by swinging on its cord. It has hardened itself in the air, that luxurious eiderdown. It now plunges into the stern realities of life.

I see a thousand dangers ahead of it. The merest breath of wind could blow it on to the hard rock, or into the stagnant water in some deep cart-rut, or on the sand where nothing grows, or else on a clay soil, too tough for it to dig in.

The feeble creature needs shelter at once, and must look for an underground refuge. The days are growing cold, and delays are fatal to it. It must wander about in search of soft soil, and no doubt many die before they find it.

When at last it discovers the right spot it attacks the earth with the hooks on its fore-feet. Through the magnifying-glass I watch it wielding its pickaxes, and raking an atom of earth to the surface. In a few minutes a well has been scooped out. The little creature goes down into it, buries itself, and is henceforth invisible.

The underground life of the undeveloped Cicada remains a secret. But we know how long it remains in the earth before it comes to the surface and becomes a full-grown Cicada. For four years it lives below the soil. Then for about five weeks it sings in the sunshine.

Four years of hard work in the darkness, and a month of delight in the sun—such is the Cicada's life. We must not blame him for the noisy triumph of his song. For four years he has dug the earth with his feet, and then suddenly he is dressed in exquisite raiment, provided with wings that rival the bird's, and bathed in heat and light! What cymbals can be loud enough to celebrate his happiness, so hardly earned, and so very, very short?

CHAPTER IV

The Praying Mantis

I

Her Hunting

There is an insect of the south that is quite as interesting as the Cicada, but much less famous, because it makes no noise. Had it been provided with cymbals, its renown would have been greater than the celebrated musician's, for it is most unusual both in shape and habits.

A long time ago, in the days of ancient Greece, this insect was named Mantis, or the Prophet. The peasant saw her on the sun-scorched grass, standing half-erect in a very imposing and majestic manner, with her broad green gossamer wings trailing like long veils, and her fore-legs, like arms, raised to the sky as though in prayer. To the peasant's ignorance the insect seemed like a priestess or a nun, and so she came to be called the Praying Mantis.

There was never a greater mistake! Those pious airs are a fraud; those arms raised in prayer are really the most horrible weapons, which slay whatever passes within reach. The Mantis is fierce as a tigress, cruel as an ogress. She feeds only on living creatures.

There is nothing in her appearance to inspire dread. She is not without a certain beauty, with her slender, graceful figure, her pale-green colouring, and her long gauze wings. Having a flexible neck, she can move her head freely in all directions. She is the only insect that can direct her gaze wherever she will. She almost has a face.

Great is the contrast between this peaceful-looking body and the murderous machinery of the fore-legs. The haunch is very long and powerful, while the thigh is even longer, and carries on

24

its lower surface two rows of sharp spikes or teeth. Behind these teeth are three spurs. In short, the thigh is a saw with two blades, between which the leg lies when folded back.

This leg itself is also a double-edged saw, provided with a greater number of teeth than the thigh. It ends in a strong hook with a point as sharp as a needle, and a double blade like a curved pruning-knife. I have many painful memories of this hook. Many a time, when Mantis-hunting, I have been clawed by the insect and forced to ask somebody else to release me. No insect in this part of the world is so troublesome to handle. The Mantis claws you with her pruning-hooks, pricks you with her spikes, seizes you in her vice, and makes self-defence impossible if you wish to keep your captive alive.

When at rest, the trap is folded back against the chest and looks quite harmless. There you have the insect praying. But if a victim passes by, the appearance of prayer is quickly dropped. The three long divisions of the trap are suddenly unfolded, and the prey is caught with the sharp hook at the end of them, and drawn back between the two saws. Then the vice closes, and all is over. Locusts, Grasshoppers, and even stronger insects are helpless against the four rows of teeth.

It is impossible to make a complete study of the habits of the Mantis in the open fields, so I am obliged to take her indoors. She can live quite happily in a pan filled with sand and covered with a gauze dish-cover, if only she be supplied with plenty of fresh food. In order to find out what can be done by the strength and daring of the Mantis, I provide her not only with Locusts and Grasshoppers, but also with the largest Spiders of the neighbourhood. This is what I see.

A grey Locust, heedless of danger, walks towards the Mantis. The latter gives a convulsive shiver, and suddenly, in the most surprising way, strikes an attitude that fills the Locust with terror, and is quite enough to startle any one. You see before you unexpectedly a sort of bogy-man or Jack-in-the-box. The wing-covers open; the wings spread to their full extent and stand erect like sails, towering over the insect's back; the tip of the body curls up like a crook, rising and falling with short jerks, and making a sound like the puffing of a startled Adder. Planted defiantly on its four hind-legs, the Mantis holds the front part of its body almost upright. The murderous legs open wide, and show a pattern of black-and-white spots beneath them.

In this strange attitude the Mantis stands motionless, with eyes fixed on her prey. If the Locust moves, the Mantis turns her head. The object of this performance is plain. It is intended to strike terror into the heart of the victim, to paralyse it with fright before attacking it. The Mantis is pretending to be a ghost!

The plan is quite successful. The Locust sees a spectre before him, and gazes at it without moving. He to whom leaping is so easy makes no attempt at escape. He stays stupidly where he is, or even draws nearer with a leisurely step.

As soon as he is within reach of the Mantis she strikes with her claws; her double saws close and clutch; the poor wretch protests in vain; the cruel ogress begins her meal.

The pretty Crab Spider stabs her victim in the neck, in order to poison it and make it helpless. In the same way the Mantis attacks the Locust first at the back of the neck, to destroy its power of movement. This enables her to kill and eat an insect as big as herself, or even bigger. It is amazing that the greedy creature can contain so much food.

The various Digger-wasps receive visits from her pretty frequently. Posted near the burrows on a bramble, she waits for chance to bring near her a double prize, the Hunting-wasp and the prey she is bringing home. For a long time she waits in vain; for the Wasp is suspicious and on her guard: still, now and then a rash one is caught. With a sudden rustle of wings the Mantis terrifies the new-comer, who hesitates for a moment in her fright. Then, with the sharpness of a spring, the Wasp is fixed as in a trap between the blades of the double saw—the toothed fore-arm and toothed upper-arm of the Mantis. The victim is then gnawed in small mouthfuls.

I once saw a Bee-eating Wasp, while carrying a Bee to her storehouse, attacked and caught by a Mantis. The Wasp was in the act of eating the honey she had found in the Bee's crop. The double saw of the Mantis closed suddenly on the feasting Wasp; but neither terror nor torture could persuade that greedy creature to leave off eating. Even while she was herself being actually devoured she continued to lick the honey from her Bee!

I regret to say that the meals of this savage ogress are not confined to other kinds of insects. For all her sanctimonious airs she is a cannibal. She will eat her sister as calmly as though she were a Grasshopper; and those around her will make no protest, being quite ready to do the same on the first opportunity. Indeed, she even makes a habit of devouring her mate, whom she seizes by the neck and then swallows by little mouthfuls, leaving only the wings.

She is worse than the Wolf; for it is said that even Wolves never eat each other.

II

Her Nest

After all, however, the Mantis has her good points, like most people. She makes a most marvellous nest.

This nest is to be found more or less everywhere in sunny places: on stones, wood, vine-stocks, twigs, or dry grass, and even on such things as bits of brick, strips of linen, or the shrivelled leather of an old boot. Any support will serve, as long as there is an uneven surface to form a solid foundation.

In size the nest is between one and two inches long, and less than an inch wide; and its colour is as golden as a grain of wheat. It is made of a frothy substance, which has become solid and hard, and it smells like silk when it is burnt. The shape of it varies according to the support on which it is based, but in all cases the upper surface is convex. One can distinguish three bands, or zones, of which the middle one is made of little plates or scales, arranged in pairs and over-lapping like the tiles of a roof. The edges of these plates are free, forming two rows of slits or little doorways, through which the young Mantis escapes at the moment of hatching. In every other part the wall of the nest is impenetrable.

The eggs are arranged in layers, with the ends containing the heads pointed towards the doorways. Of these doorways, as I

have just said, there are two rows. One half of the grubs will go
out through the right door, and the other half through the left.

It is a remarkable fact that the mother Mantis builds this
cleverly-made nest while she is actually laying her eggs. From
her body she produces a sticky substance, rather like the
Caterpillar's silk-fluid; and this material she mixes with the air
and whips into froth. She beats it into foam with two ladles that
she has at the tip of her body, just as we beat white of egg with
a fork. The foam is greyish-white, almost like soapsuds, and
when it first appears it is sticky; but two minutes afterwards it
has solidified.

In this sea of foam the Mantis deposits her eggs. As each layer
of eggs is laid, it is covered with froth, which quickly becomes
solid.

In a new nest the belt of exit-doors is coated with a material
that seems different from the rest—a layer of fine porous matter, of a pure, dull, almost chalky white, which contrasts with the
dirty white of the remainder of the nest. It is like the mixture
that confectioners make of whipped white of egg, sugar, and
starch, with which to ornament their cakes. This snowy covering
is very easily crumbled and removed. When it is gone the exit-
belt is clearly visible, with its two rows of plates. The wind and
rain sooner or later remove it in strips or flakes, and therefore
the old nests show no traces of it.

But these two materials, though they appear different, are
really only two forms of the same matter. The Mantis with her
ladles sweeps the surface of the foam, skimming the top of the
froth, and collecting it into a band along the back of the nest.
The ribbon that looks like sugar-icing is merely the thinnest and
lightest portion of the sticky spray, which appears whiter than
the nest because its bubbles are more delicate, and reflect more
light.

It is truly a wonderful piece of machinery that can, so
methodically and swiftly, produce the horny central substance
on which the first eggs are laid, the eggs themselves, the protecting froth, the soft sugar-like covering of the doorways, and at
the same time can build overlapping plates, and the narrow passages leading to them! Yet the Mantis, while she is doing all this,

hangs motionless on the foundation of the nest. She gives not a glance at the building that is rising behind her. Her legs act no part in the affair. The machinery works by itself.

As soon as she has done her work the mother withdraws. I expected to see her return and show some tender feeling for the cradle of her family, but it evidently has no further interest for her.

The Mantis, I fear, has no heart. She eats her husband, and deserts her children.

III

The Hatching of Her Eggs

The eggs of the Mantis usually hatch in bright sunshine, at about ten o'clock on a mid-June morning.

As I have already told you, there is only one part of the nest from which the grub can find an outlet, namely the band of scales round the middle. From under each of these scales one sees slowly appearing a blunt, transparent lump, followed by two large black specks, which are the creature's eyes. The baby grub slips gently under the thin plate and half releases itself. It is reddish yellow, and has a thick, swollen head. Under its outer skin it is quite easy to distinguish the large black eyes, the mouth flattened against the chest, the legs plastered to the body from front to back. With the exception of the legs the whole thing reminds one somewhat of the first state of the Cicada on leaving the egg.

Like the Cicada, the young Mantis finds it necessary to wear an overall when it is coming into the world, for the sake of convenience and safety. It has to emerge from the depths of the nest through narrow, winding ways, in which full-spread slender limbs could not find enough room. The tall stilts, the murderous harpoons, the delicate antennæ, would hinder its passage, and indeed make it impossible. The creature therefore appears in swaddling-clothes, and has the shape of a boat.

When the grub peeps out under the thin scales of its nest its head becomes bigger and bigger, till it looks like a throbbing blister. The little creature alternately pushes forward and draws back, in its efforts to free itself, and at each movement the head grows larger. At last the outer skin bursts at the upper part of the chest, and the grub wriggles and tugs and bends about, determined to throw off its overall. Finally the legs and the long antennæ are freed, and a few shakes complete the operation.

It is a striking sight to see a hundred young Mantes coming from the nest at once. Hardly does one tiny creature show its black eyes under a scale before a swarm of others appears. It is as though a signal passed from one to the other, so swiftly does the hatching spread. Almost in a moment the middle zone of the nest is covered with grubs, who run about feverishly, stripping themselves of their torn garments. Then they drop off, or clamber into the nearest foliage. A few days later a fresh swarm appears, and so on till all the eggs are hatched.

But alas! the poor grubs are hatched into a world of dangers. I have seen them hatching many times, both out of doors in my enclosure, and in the seclusion of a greenhouse, where I hoped I should be better able to protect them. Twenty times at least I have watched the scene, and every time the slaughter of the grubs has been terrible. The Mantis lays many eggs, but she will never lay enough to cope with the hungry murderers who lie in wait until the grubs appear.

The Ants, above all, are their enemies. Every day I find them visiting my nests. It is in vain for me to interfere; they always get the better of me. They seldom succeed in entering the nest; its hard walls form too strong a fortress. But they wait outside for their prey.

The moment that the young grubs appear they are grabbed by the Ants, pulled out of their sheaths, and cut in pieces. You see piteous struggles between the little creatures who can only protest with wild wrigglings and the ferocious brigands who are carrying them off. In a moment the massacre is over; all that is left of the flourishing family is a few scattered survivors who have escaped by accident.

It is curious that the Mantis, the scourge of the insect race, should be herself so often devoured at this early stage of her life, by one of the least of that race, the Ant. The ogress sees her family eaten by the dwarf. But this does not continue long. So soon as she has become firm and strong from contact with the air the Mantis can hold her own. She trots about briskly among the Ants, who fall back as she passes, no longer daring to tackle her: with her fore-legs brought close to her chest, like arms ready for self-defence, she already strikes awe into them by her proud bearing.

But the Mantis has another enemy who is less easily dismayed. The little Grey Lizard, the lover of sunny walls, pays small heed to threatening attitudes. With the tip of his slender tongue he picks up, one by one, the few stray insects that have escaped the Ant. They make but a small mouthful, but to judge from the Lizard's expression they taste very good. Every time he gulps down one of the little creatures he half-closes his eyelids, a sign of profound satisfaction.

Moreover, even before the hatching the eggs are in danger. There is a tiny insect called the Chalcis, who carries a probe sharp enough to penetrate the nest of solidified foam. So the brood of the Mantis shares the fate of the Cicada's. The eggs of a stranger are laid in the nest, and are hatched before those of the rightful owner. The owner's eggs are then eaten by the invaders. The Mantis lays, perhaps, a thousand eggs. Possibly only one couple of these escapes destruction.

The Mantis eats the Locust: the Ant eats the Mantis: the Wryneck eats the Ant. And in the autumn, when the Wryneck has grown fat from eating many Ants, I eat the Wryneck.

It may well be that the Mantis, the Locust, the Ant, and even lesser creatures contribute to the strength of the human brain. In strange and unseen ways they have all supplied a drop of oil to feed the lamp of thought. Their energies, slowly developed, stored up, and handed on to us, pass into our veins and sustain our weakness. We live by their death. The world is an endless circle. Everything finishes so that everything may begin again; everything dies so that everything may live.

In many ages the Mantis has been regarded with superstitious awe. In Provence its nest is held to be the best remedy for chilblains. You cut the thing in two, squeeze it, and rub the afflicted part with the juice that streams out of it. The peasants declare that it works like a charm. I have never felt any relief from it myself.

Further, it is highly praised as a wonderful cure for toothache. As long as you have it on you, you need never fear that trouble. Our housewives gather it under a favourable moon; they keep it carefully in the corner of a cupboard, or sew it into their pocket. The neighbours borrow it when tortured by a tooth. They call it a *tigno*.

"Lend me your *tigno*; I am in agony," says the sufferer with the swollen face.

The other hastens to unstitch and hand over the precious thing.

"Don't lose it, whatever you do," she says earnestly to her friend. "It's the only one I have, and this isn't the right time of moon."

This simplicity of our peasants is surpassed by an English physician and man of science who lived in the sixteenth century. He tells us that, in those days, if a child lost his way in the country, he would ask the Mantis to put him on his road. "The Mantis," adds the author, "will stretch out one of her feet and shew him the right way and seldome or never misse."

CHAPTER V

The Glow-Worm

I

His Surgical Instrument

Few insects enjoy more fame then the Glow-worm, the curious little animal who celebrates the joy of life by lighting a lantern at its tail-end. We all know it, at least by name, even if we have not seen it roaming through the grass, like a spark fallen from the full moon. The Greeks of old called it the Bright-tailed, and modern science gives it the name *Lampyris.*

As a matter of fact the Lampyris is not a worm at all, not even in general appearance. He has six short legs, which he well knows how to use, for he is a real gad-about. The male, when he is full-grown has wingcases, like the true Beetle that he is. The female is an unattractive creature who knows nothing of the delights of flying and all her life remains in the *larva,* or incomplete form. Even at this stage the word "worm" is out of place. We French use the phrase "naked as a worm" to express the lack of any kind of protection. Now the Lampyris is clothed, that is to say he wears an outer skin that serves as a defence; and he is, moreover, rather richly coloured. He is dark brown, with pale pink on the chest; and each segment, or division, of his body is ornamented at the edge with two spots of fairly bright red. A costume like this was never worn by a worm!

Nevertheless we will continue to call him the Glow-worm, since it is by that name that he is best known to the world.

The two most interesting peculiarities about the Glow-worm are, first, the way he secures his food, and secondly, the lantern at his tail.

A famous Frenchman, a master of the science of food, once said:

"Show me what you eat, and I will tell you what you are."

A similar question should be addressed to every insect whose habits we propose to study; for the information supplied by food is the chief of all the documents of animal life. Well, in spite of his innocent appearance, the Glow-worm is an eater of flesh, a hunter of game; and he carries on his hunting with rare villainy. His regular prey is the Snail. This fact has long been known; but what is not so well known is his curious method of attack, of which I have seen no other example anywhere.

Before he begins to feed on his victim he gives it an anæsthetic—he makes it unconscious, as a person is made unconscious with chloroform before a surgical operation. His food, as a rule, is a certain small Snail hardly the size of a cherry, which collects in clusters during the hot weather, on the stiff stubble and other dry stalks by the roadside, and there remains motionless, in profound meditation, throughout the scorching summer days. In some such place as this I have often seen the Glow-worm feasting on his unconscious prey, which he had just paralysed on its shaky support.

But he frequents other places too. At the edge of cool, damp ditches, where the vegetation is varied, many Snails are to be found; and in such spots as these the Glow-worm can kill his victim on the ground. I can reproduce these conditions at home, and can there follow the operator's performance down to the smallest detail.

I will try to describe the strange sight. I place a little grass in a wide glass jar. In this I install a few Glow-worms and a supply of Snails of a suitable size, neither too large nor too small. One must be patient and wait, and above all keep a careful watch, for the events take place unexpectedly and do not last long.

For a moment the Glow-worm examines his prey, which, according to its habit, is completely hidden in the shell, except for the edge of the "mantle," which projects slightly. Then the hunter draws his weapon. It is a very simple weapon, but it cannot be seen without a magnifying-glass. It consists of two mandibles, bent back into a hook, very sharp and as thin as a hair. Through the microscope one can see a slender groove running down the hook. And that is all.

The insect repeatedly taps the Snail's mantle with its instrument. It all happens with such gentleness as to suggest kisses
rather than bites. As children, teasing one another, we used to
talk of "tweaks" to express a slight squeeze of the finger-tips,
something more like tickling than a serious pinch. Let us use
that word. In conversation with animals, language loses nothing
by remaining simple. The Glow-worm gives tweaks to the Snail.

He doles them out methodically, without hurrying, and takes
a brief rest after each of them, as though to find out what effect
has been produced. The number of tweaks is not great: half a
dozen at most, which are enough to make the Snail motionless,
and to rob him of all feeling. That other pinches are administered later, at the time of eating, seems very likely, but I cannot
say anything for certain on that subject. The first few, however—there are never many—are enough to prevent the Snail
from feeling anything, thanks to the promptitude of the Glow-
worm, who, at lightning speed, darts some kind of poison into
his victim by means of his grooved hooks.

There is no doubt at all that the Snail is made insensible to
pain. If, when the Glow-worm has dealt some four or five of his
twitches, I take away the victim and prick it with a fine needle,
there is not a quiver in the wounded flesh, there is not the smallest sign of life. Moreover, I occasionally chance to see Snails
attacked by the Lampyris while they are creeping along the
ground, the foot slowly crawling, the tentacles swollen to their
full extent. A few disordered movements betray a brief excitement on the part of the Snail, and then everything ceases: the
foot no longer crawls, the front-part loses its graceful curve, the
tentacles become limp and give way under their own weight,
dangling feebly like a broken stick. The Snail, to all appearance,
is dead.

He is not, however, really dead. I can bring him to life again.
When he has been for two or three days in a condition that is
neither life nor death I give him a shower-bath. In about a couple of days my prisoner, so lately injured by the Glow-worm's
treachery, is restored to his usual state. He revives, he recovers
movement and sensibility. He is affected by the touch of a needle; he shifts his place, crawls, puts out his tentacles, as though

nothing unusual had occurred. The general torpor, a sort of deep drunkenness, has vanished outright. The dead returns to life.

Human science did not invent the art of making a person insensible to pain, which is one of the triumphs of surgery. Far back in the centuries the Glow-worm, and apparently others too, was practising it. The surgeon makes us breathe the fumes of ether or chloroform: the insect darts forth from his fangs very tiny doses of a special poison.

When we consider the harmless and peaceful nature of the Snail it seems curious that the Glow-worm should require this remarkable talent. But I think I know the reason.

When the Snail is on the ground, creeping, or even shrunk into his shell, the attack never presents any difficulty. The shell possesses no lid and leaves the hermit's fore-part to a great extent exposed. But it very often happens that he is in a raised position, clinging to the tip of a grass-stalk, or perhaps to the smooth surface of a stone. This support to which he fastens himself serves very well as a protection; it acts as a lid, supposing that the shell fits closely on the stone or stalk. But if the least bit of the Snail be left uncovered the slender hooks of the Glow-worm can find their way in through the gap, and in a moment the victim is made unconscious, and can be eaten in comfort.

Now, a Snail perched on top of a stalk is very easily upset. The slightest struggle, the most feeble wriggle on his part, would dislodge him; he would fall to the ground, and the Glow-worm would be left without food. It is necessary for the Snail to be made instantly unconscious of pain, or he would escape; and it must be done with a touch so delicate that it does not shake him from his stalk. And that, I think, is why the Glow-worm possesses his strange surgical instrument.

II

His Rosette

The Glow-worm not only makes his victim insensible while he is poised on the side of a dry grass-stalk, but he eats him in the same dangerous position. And his preparations for his meal are by no means simple.

What is his manner of consuming it? Does he really eat, that is to say, does he divide his food into pieces, does he carve it into minute particles, which are afterwards ground by a chewing-apparatus? I think not. I never see a trace of solid nourishment on my captives' mouths. The Glow-worm does not eat in the strict sense of the word; he merely drinks. He feeds on a thin gruel, into which he transforms his prey. Like the flesh-eating grub of the Fly, he can digest his food before he swallows it; he turns his prey into liquid before feeding on it.

This is how things happen. A Snail has been made insensible by a Glow-worm, who is nearly always alone, even when the prize is a large one like the Common Snail. Soon a number of guests hasten up—two, three, or more—and, without any quarrel with the real owner, all alike fall to. A couple of days later, if I turn the shell so that the opening is downwards, the contents flow out like soup from a saucepan. By the time the meal is finished only insignificant remains are left.

The matter is obvious. By repeated tiny bites, similar to the tweaks which we saw administered at the beginning, the flesh of the Snail is converted into a gruel on which the various guests nourish themselves each in his own way, each working at the broth by means of some special pepsine (or digestive fluid), and each taking his own mouthfuls of it. The use of this method shows that the Glow-worm's mouth must be very feebly armed, apart from the two fangs which sting the patient and inject the poison. No doubt these fangs at the same time inject some other substance which turns the solid flesh into liquid, in such a thorough way that every morsel is turned to account.

And this is done with exquisite delicacy, though sometimes in a position that is anything but steady. The Snails imprisoned in my apparatus sometimes crawl up to the top, which is closed with a glass pane. To this pane they fix themselves with a speck of the sticky substance they carry with them; but, as they are miserly in their use of this substance, the merest shake is enough to loosen the shell and send it to the bottom of the jar.

Now it is not unusual for the Glow-worm to hoist himself to

the top, with the help of a certain climbing-organ that makes up
for the weakness of his legs. He selects his prey, makes a careful
inspection of it to find a slit, nibbles it a little, makes it insensible, and then, without delay, proceeds to prepare the gruel
which he will go on eating for days on end.

When he has finished his meal the shell is found to be
absolutely empty. And yet this shell, which was fixed to the glass
only by the slight smear of stickiness, has not come loose, nor
even shifted its position in the smallest degree. Without any
protest from the hermit who has been gradually converted into
broth, it has been drained dry on the very spot at which the first
attack was made. These small details show us how promptly the
anæsthetic bite takes effect, and how very skilfully the Glow-
worm treats his Snail.

To do all this, poised high in air on a sheet of glass or a grass-
stem, the Glow-worm must have some special limb or organ to
keep him from slipping. It is plain that his short clumsy legs are
not enough.

Through the magnifying-glass we can see that he does indeed
possess a special organ of this kind. Beneath his body, towards
the tail, there is a white spot. The glass shows that this is composed of about a dozen short, fleshy little tubes, or stumpy fingers, which are sometimes gathered into a cluster, sometimes
spread into a rosette. This bunch of little fingers helps the Glow-
worm to stick to a smooth surface, and also to climb. If he wishes to fix himself to a pane of glass or a stalk he opens his rosette,
and spreads it wide on the support, to which it clings by its own
natural stickiness. And by opening and shutting alternately it
helps him to creep along and to climb.

The little fingers that form this rosette are not jointed, but are
able to move in all directions. Indeed they are more like tubes
than fingers, for they cannot seize anything, they can only hold
on by their stickiness. They are very useful, however, for they
have a third purpose, besides their powers of clinging and
climbing. They are used as a sponge and brush. At a moment of
rest, after a meal, the Glow-worm passes and repasses this brush
over his head and sides and his whole body, a performance made
possible by the flexibility of his spine. This is done point by

point, from one end of the body to the other, with a scrupulous care that proves the great interest he takes in the operation. At first one may wonder why he should dust and polish himself so carefully. But no doubt, by the time he has turned the Snail into gruel inside the shell and has then spent several days in eating the result of his labours, a wash and brush-up is not amiss.

III

His Lamp

If the Glow-worm possessed no other talent than that of chloroforming his prey by means of a few tweaks as gentle as kisses, he would be unknown to the world in general. But he also knows how to light himself like a lantern. He shines; which is an excellent manner of becoming famous.

In the case of the female Glow-worm the lighting-apparatus occupies the last three divisions of the body. On each of the first two it takes the form, on the under surface, of a wide belt of light; on the third division or segment the bright part is much smaller, and consists only of two spots, which shine through the back, and are visible both above and below the animal. From these belts and spots there comes a glorious white light, delicately tinged with blue.

The male Glow-worm carries only the smaller of these lamps, the two spots on the end segment, which are possessed by the entire tribe. These luminous spots appear upon the young grub, and continue throughout life unchanged. And they are always visible both on the upper and lower surface, whereas the two large belts peculiar to the female shine only below the body.

I have examined the shining belt under the microscope. On the skin a sort of whitewash is spread, formed of some very fine grain-like substance, which is the source of the light. Close beside it is a curious air-tube, with a short wide stem leading to a kind of bushy tuft of delicate branches. These branches spread over the sheet of shining matter, and sometimes dip into it.

It is plain to me that the brightness is produced by the breathing-organs of the Glow-worm. There are certain substances which, when mixed with air, become luminous or even burst

into flame. Such substances are called *combustible,* and the act
of their producing light or flame by mingling with the air is
called *oxidisation.* The lamp of the Glow-worm is the result of
oxidisation. The substance that looks like whitewash is the matter that is oxidised, and the air is supplied by the tube connected with the Glow-worm's breathing-organs. But as to the nature
of the shining substance, no one as yet knows anything.

We are better informed as regards another question. We
know that the Glow-worm has complete control of the light he
carries. He can turn it up or down, or out, as he pleases.

If the flow of air through the tube be increased, the light
becomes more intense: if the same air-tube, influenced by the
will of the animal, stops the passage of air, the light grows fainter
or even goes out.

Excitement produces an effect upon the air-tube. I am speak-
ing now of the modest fairy-lamp, the spots on the last segment
of the Glow-worm's body. These are suddenly and almost completely put out by any kind of flurry. When I am hunting for
young Glow-worms I can plainly see them glimmering on the
blades of grass; but should the least false step disturb a neighbouring twig, the light goes out at once and the insect becomes
invisible.

The gorgeous belts of the females, however, are very little, if
at all, affected by even the most violent surprise. I fire a gun, for
instance, beside a wire-gauze cage in which I am rearing a
menagerie of female Glow-worms in the open air. The explosion
produces no result: the illumination continues, as bright and
placid as before. I take a spray, and rain down a slight shower of
cold water upon the flock. Not one of my animals puts out its
light; at the very most there is a brief pause in the radiance, and
then only in some cases. I send a puff of smoke from my pipe
into the cage. This time the pause is more marked. There are
even some lamps put out, but they are soon relit. Calm returns,
and the light is as bright as ever. I take some of the captives in
my fingers and tease them a little. Yet the illumination is not
much dimmed, if I do not press too hard with my thumb.
Nothing short of very serious reasons would make the insect put
out its signals altogether.

All things considered, there is not a doubt but that the Glow-worm himself manages his lighting-apparatus, extinguishing and rekindling it at will; but there is one circumstance over which the insect has no control. If I cut off a strip of the skin, showing one of the luminous belts, and place it in a glass tube, it will shine away merrily, though not quite as brilliantly as on the living body. The presence of life is unnecessary, because the luminous skin is in direct contact with the air, and the flow of oxygen through the air-tube is therefore not required. In aerated water the skin shines as brightly as in the free air, but the light is extinguished in water that has been deprived of its air by boiling. There could be no better proof that the Glow-worm's light is the effect of oxidisation.

The light is white, calm, and soft to the eyes, and suggests a spark dropped by the full moon. In spite of its splendour it is very feeble. If we move a Glow-worm along a line of print, in perfect darkness, we can easily make out the letters one by one, and even words when they are not too long; but nothing is visible beyond this very narrow zone. A lantern of this kind soon tires the reader's patience.

These brilliant creatures know nothing at all of family affection. They lay their eggs anywhere, or rather strew them at random, either on the earth or on a blade of grass. Then they pay no further attention to them.

From start to finish the Glow-worm shines. Even the eggs are luminous, and so are the grubs. At the approach of cold weather the latter go down into the ground, but not very far. If I dig them up I find them with their little stern-lights still shining. Even below the soil they keep their lanterns bravely alight.

CHAPTER VI

A Mason-Wasp

I

Her Choice of a Building-Site

Of the various insects that like to make their home in our houses, certainly the most interesting, for her beautiful shape, her curious manners, and her wonderful nest, is a certain Wasp called the Pelopæus. She is very little known, even to the people by whose fireside she lives. This is owing to her quiet, peaceful ways; she is so very retiring that her host is nearly always ignorant of her presence. It is easy for noisy, tiresome, unpleasant persons to make themselves famous. I will try to rescue this modest creature from her obscurity.

The Pelopæus is an extremely chilly mortal. She pitches her tent under the kindly sun that ripens the olive and prompts the Cicada's song; and even then she needs for her family the additional warmth to be found in our dwellings. Her usual refuge is the peasant's lonely cottage, with its old fig-tree shading the well in front of the door. She chooses one exposed to all the heat of summers, and if possible possessing a big fireplace in which a fire of sticks always burns. The cheerful blaze on winter evenings has a great influence upon her choice, for she knows by the blackness of the chimney that the spot is a likely one. A chimney that is not well glazed by smoke gives her no confidence: people must shiver with cold in that house.

During the dog-days in July and August the visitor suddenly appears, seeking a place for her nest. She is not in the least disturbed by the bustle and movement of the household: they take no notice of her nor she of them. She examines—now with her sharp eyes, now with her sensitive antennæ—the corners of the blackened ceiling, the rafters, the chimney-piece, the sides of the fireplace especially, and even the inside of the flue. Having finished her inspection and duly approved of the site she flies away, soon to return with the pellet of mud which will form the first layer of the building.

The spot she chooses varies greatly, and often it is a very curious one. The temperature of a furnace appears to suit the young Pelopæus: at least the favourite site is the chimney, on either side of the flue, up to a height of twenty inches or so. This snug shelter has its drawbacks. The smoke gets to the nests, and gives them a glaze of brown or black like that which covers the stonework. They might easily be taken for inequalities in the mortar. This is not a serious matter, provided that the flames do not lick against the nests. That would stew the young Wasps to death in their clay pots. But the mother Wasp seems to understand this: she only places her family in chimneys that are too wide for anything but smoke to reach their sides.

But in spite of all her caution one danger remains. It sometimes happens, while the Wasp is building, that the approach to the half-built dwelling is barred to her for a time, or even for the whole day, by a curtain of steam or smoke. Washing-days are most risky. From morning till night the housewife keeps the huge cauldron boiling. The smoke from the hearth, the steam from the cauldron and the wash-tub, form a dense mist in front of the fireplace.

It is told of the Water-Ouzel that, to get back to his nest, he will fly through the cataract under a mill-weir. This wasp is even more daring: with her pellet of mud in her teeth she crosses the cloud of smoke and disappears behind it, where she becomes invisible, so thick is the screen. An irregular chirring sound, the song she sings at her work, alone betrays her presence. The building goes on mysteriously behind the cloud. The song ceases, and the Wasp flies back through the steam, quite unharmed. She will face this danger repeatedly all day, until the cell is built, stored with food, and closed.

Once and once only I was able to observe a Pelopæus at my own fireside; and, as it happened, it was a washing-day. I had not long been appointed to the Avignon grammar-school. It was close upon two o'clock, and in a few minutes the roll of the

drum would summon me to give a scientific lecture to an audi-
ence of wool-gatherers. Suddenly I saw a strange, agile insect
dart through the steam that rose from the wash-tub. The front
part of its body was very thin, and the back part was very plump,
and the two parts were joined together by a long thread. It was
the Pelopæus, the first I had seen with observant eyes.

Being very anxious to become better acquainted with my visitor, I fervently entreated the household not to disturb her in
my absence. Things went better than I dared hope. On my
return she was still carrying on her mason's work behind the
steam. Being eager to see the building of the cells, the nature
of the provisions, and the evolution of the young Wasps, I raked
the fire so as to decrease the volume of smoke, and for a good
two hours I watched the mother Wasp diving through the
cloud.

Never again, in the forty years that followed, was my fireplace
honoured with such a visit. All the further information I have
gathered was gleaned on the hearths of my neighbours.

The Pelopæus, it appears, is of a solitary and vagrant disposi-
tion. She nearly always builds a lonely nest, and unlike many
Wasps and Bees, she seldom founds her family at the spot where
she was reared herself. She is often found in our southern
towns, but on the whole she prefers the peasant's smoky house
to the townsman's white villa. Nowhere have I seen her so plentiful as in my village, with its tumble-down cottages burnt yellow
by the sun.

It is obvious that this Wasp, when she so often chooses the
chimney as her abode, is not seeking her own comfort: the site
means work, and dangerous work. She seeks the welfare of her
family. This family, then, must require a high temperature, such
as other Wasps and Bees do not need.

I have seen a Pelopæus nest in the engine-room of a silk-fac-
tory, fixed to the ceiling just above the huge boiler. At this spot
the thermometer marked 120 degrees all through the year,
except at night and on holidays.

In a country distillery I have found many nests, fixed on anything that came to hand, even a pile of account-books. The temperature of one of these, quite close to the still, was 113 degrees.

It is plain that this Wasp cheerfully endures a degree of heat that makes the oily palm-tree sprout.

A boiler or a furnace she regards as the ideal home, but she is quite willing to content herself in any snug corner: a conservatory, a kitchen-ceiling, the recess of a closed window, the wall of a cottage bedroom. As to the foundation on which she fixes her nest, she is entirely indifferent. As a rule she builds her groups of cells on stonework or timber; but at various times I have seen nests inside a gourd, in a fur cap, in the hollow of a brick, on the side of a bag of oats, and in a piece of lead tubing.

Once I saw something more remarkable still, in a farm near Avignon. In a large room with a very wide fireplace the soup for the farm-hands and the food for the cattle simmered in a row of pots. The labourers used to come in from the fields to this room, and devour their meal with the silent haste that comes from a keen appetite. To enjoy this half-hour comfortably they would take off their hats and smocks, and hang them on pegs. Short though this meal was, it was long enough to allow the Wasps to take possession of their garments. The inside of a straw hat was recognised as a most useful building-site, the folds of a smock were looked upon as a capital shelter; and the work of building started at once. On rising from the table one of the men would shake his smock, and another his hat, to rid it of the Wasp's nest, which was already the size of an acorn.

The cook in that farmhouse regarded the Wasps with no friendly eye. They dirtied everything, she said. Dabs of mud on the ceiling, on the walls, or on the chimney-piece you could put up with; but it was a very different matter when you found them on the linen and the curtains. She had to beat the curtains every day with a bamboo. And it was trouble thrown away. The next morning the Wasps began building as busily as ever.

II

Her Building

I sympathised with the sorrows of that farm-cook, but greatly regretted that I could not take her place. How gladly I would have left the Wasps undisturbed, even if they had covered all the

furniture with mud! How I longed to know what the fate of a
nest would be, if perched on the uncertain support of a coat or
a curtain! The nest of the Mason-bee is made of hard mortar,
which surrounds the twig on which it is built, and becomes firmly fixed to it; but the nest of the Pelopæus Wasp is a mere blob
of mud, without cement or foundations.

The materials of which it is made are nothing but wet earth
or dirt, picked up wherever the soil is damp enough. The thin
clay of a river-bank is very suitable, but in my stony country
streams are rare. I can, however, watch the builders at my
leisure in my own garden, when a thin trickle of water runs all
day, as it does sometimes, through the little trenches that are cut
in my vegetable plots.

The Pelopæus Wasps of the neighbourhood soon become
aware of this glad event, and come hurrying up to take advantage of the precious layer of mud, a rare discovery in the dry season. They scrape and skim the gleaming, shiny surface with their
mandibles while standing high on their legs, with their wings
quivering and their black bodies upraised. No neat little housewife, with skirts carefully tucked up out of the dirt, could be
more skilful in tackling a job likely to soil her clothes. These
mud-gatherers have not an atom of dirt upon them, so careful
are they to tuck up their skirts in their own fashion, that is to say,
to keep their whole body out of the way, all but the tips of their
legs and the busy points of the mandibles with which they work.

In this way a dab of mud is collected, almost the size of a pea.
Taking the load in its teeth the insect flies off, adds a layer to its
building, and soon returns to collect another pellet. The same
method is pursued as long as the earth remains sufficiently wet,
during the hottest hours of the day.

But the favourite spot is the great fountain in the village,
where the people come to water their mules. Here there is a
constant sheet of black mud which neither the hottest sunshine
nor the strongest wind can dry. This bed of mire is very unpleasant for the passers-by, but the Pelopæus loves to gather her pellets here, amid the hoofs of the mules.

Unlike some builders in clay, such as the Mason-bees, the
Wasp does not improve the mud to make it into mortar, but uses

it just as it is. Consequently her nests are flimsy work, absolutely unfitted to stand the changes and chances of the open air. A drop of water laid upon their surface softens the spot touched and reduces it to mud again, while a sprinkling equal to an average shower turns it to pap. They are nothing but dried slime, and become slime again as soon as they are wetted.

It is plain, then, that even if the young Pelopæus were not so chilly by nature, a shelter is indispensable for the nests, which would go to pieces at the first shower of rain. That is why this Wasp is so fond of human dwellings, and especially of the chimney.

Before receiving its final coating, which covers up the details of the building, the nest has a certain beauty of its own. It consists of a cluster of cells, sometimes arranged side by side in a row—which makes it look rather like a mouth-organ—but more often grouped in layers placed one above the other. I have sometimes counted as many as fifteen cells; some nests contain only ten; others are reduced to three or four, or even only one.

In shape the cells are not far from cylinders, slightly larger at the mouth than at the base. They are a little more than an inch long, and about half an inch wide. Their delicate surface is carefully polished, and shows a series of string-like projections, running cross-wise, not unlike the twisted cords of some kinds of gold-lace. Each of these strings is a layer of the building; it comes from the clod of mud used for the coping of the part already built. By counting them you can tell how many journeys the Wasp has made in the course of her work. There are usually between fifteen and twenty. For one cell, therefore, the industrious builder fetches materials something like twenty times.

The mouth of the cells is, of course, always turned upwards. A pot cannot hold its contents if it be upside down. And the Wasp's cell is nothing but a pot intended to hold the store of food, a pile of small Spiders.

The cells—built one by one, stuffed full of Spiders, and closed as the eggs are laid—preserve their pretty appearance until the cluster is considered large enough. Then, to strengthen her work, the Wasp covers the whole with a casing, as a protection and defence. She lays on the plaster without stint and without art, giving it none of the delicate finishing-touches which she lavishes on the cells. The mud is applied just as it is brought, and merely spread with a few careless strokes. The beauties of the building all disappear under this ugly husk. In this final state the nest is like a great splash of mud, flung against the wall by accident.

III

Her Provisions

Now that we know what the provision-jar is like, we must find out what it contains.

The young Pelopæus is fed on Spiders. The food does not lack variety, even in the same nest and the same cell, for any Spider may form a meal, as long as it is not too large for the jar. The Cross Spider, with three crosses of white dots on her back, is the dish that occurs oftenest. I think the reason for this is simply that the Wasp does not go far from home in her hunting-trips, and the Spider with the crosses is the easiest to find.

The Spider, armed with poison-fangs, is a dangerous prey to tackle. When of fair size, she could only be conquered by a greater amount of daring and skill than the Wasp possesses. Moreover, the cells are too small to hold a bulky object. The Wasp, therefore, hunts game of moderate size. If she meets with a kind of Spider that is apt to become plump, she always chooses a young one. But, though all are small, the size of her victims varies enormously, and this variation in size leads also to variation in number. One cell will contain a dozen Spiders, while in another there are only five or six.

Another reason for her choice of small Spiders is that she kills them before putting them in her cells. She falls suddenly upon her prey, and carries it off almost without pausing in her flight. The skilful paralysis practised by some insects is unknown to her. This means that when the food is stored it soon decays. Fortunately the Spiders are small enough to be finished at a single meal. If they were large and could only be nibbled here and there, they would decay, and poison the grubs in the nest.

I always find the egg, not on the surface of the heap, but on the first Spider that was stored. There is no exception to this rule. The Wasp places a Spider at the bottom of the cell, lays her egg upon it, and then piles the other Spiders on the top. By this clever plan the grub is obliged to begin on the oldest of the dead Spiders, and then go on to the more recent. It always finds in front of it food that has not had time to decompose.

The egg is always laid on the same part of the Spider, the end containing the head being placed on the plumpest spot. This is very pleasant for the grub, for the moment it is hatched it can begin eating the tenderest and nicest food in the store. Not a mouthful is wasted, however, by these economical creatures. When the meal is finished there is practically nothing left of the whole heap of Spiders. This life of gluttony lasts for eight or ten days.

The grub then sets to work to spin its cocoon, a sack of pure, perfectly white silk, extremely delicate. Something more is required to make this sack tough enough to be a protection, so the grub produces from its body a sort of liquid varnish. As soon as it trickles into the meshes of the silk this varnish hardens, and becomes a lacquer of exquisite daintiness. The grub then fixes a hard plug at the base of the cocoon to make all secure.

When finished, the work is amber-yellow, and rather reminds one of the outer skin of an onion. It has the same fine texture, the same colour and transparency; and like the onion skin it rustles when it is fingered. From it, sooner or later according to temperature, the perfect insect is hatched.

It is possible, while the Wasp is storing her cell, to play her a trick which will show how purely mechanical her instincts are. A cell has just been completed, let us suppose, and the huntress arrives with her first Spider. She stores it away, and at once fastens her egg on the plumpest part of its body. She sets out on a second trip. I take advantage of her absence to remove with my tweezers from the bottom of the cell both the dead Spider and the egg.

The disappearance of the egg must be discovered by the Wasp, one would think, if she possesses the least gleam of intelligence. The egg is small, it is true, but it lies on a comparatively large object, the Spider. What will the Wasp do when she finds the cell empty? Will she act sensibly, and repair her loss by laying a second egg? Not at all; she behaves most absurdly.

What she does is to bring a second Spider, which she stores away with as much cheerful zeal as if nothing unfortunate had occurred. She brings a third and a fourth, and still others, each of whom I remove during her absence; so that every time she returns from the chase the storeroom is found empty. I have seen her persist obstinately for two days in seeking to fill the insatiable jar, while my patience in emptying it was equally unflagging. With the twentieth victim—possibly owing to the fatigue of so many journeys—the huntress considered that the pot was sufficiently supplied, and began most carefully to close the cell that contained absolutely nothing.

The intelligence of insects is limited everywhere in this way. The accidental difficulty which one insect is powerless to overcome, any other, no matter what its species, will be equally unable to cope with. I could give a host of similar examples to show that insects are absolutely without reasoning power, notwithstanding the wonderful perfection of their work. A long series of experiments has forced me to conclude that they are neither free nor conscious in their industry. They build, weave, hunt, stab, and paralyse their prey, in the same way as they digest their food, or secrete the poison of their sting, without the least understanding of the means or the end. They are, I am convinced, completely ignorant of their own wonderful talents.

Their instinct cannot be changed. Experience does not teach it; time does not awaken a glimmer in its unconsciousness. Pure instinct, if it stood alone, would leave the insect powerless in the face of circumstances. Yet circumstances are always changing, the unexpected is always happening. In this confusion some power is needed by the insect—as by every other creature—to teach it what to accept and what to refuse. It requires a guide of some kind, and this guide it certainly possesses. *Intelligence* is too fine a word for it: I will call it *discernment*.

Is the insect conscious of what it does? Yes, and no. No, if its action is guided by instinct. Yes, if its action is the result of discernment.

The Pelopæus, for instance, builds her cells with earth already softened into mud. This is instinct. She has always built in this way. Neither the passing ages nor the struggle for life will induce her to imitate the Mason-bee and make her nest of dry dust and cement.

This mud nest of hers needs a shelter against the rain. A hiding-place under a stone, perhaps, sufficed at first. But when she found something better she took possession of it. She installed herself in the home of man. This is discernment.

She supplies her young with food in the form of Spiders. This is instinct, and nothing will ever persuade her that young Crickets are just as good. But should there be a lack of her favourite Cross Spider she will not leave her grubs unfed; she will bring them other Spiders. This is discernment.

In this quality of discernment lies the possibility of future improvement for the insect.

IV

Her Origin

The Pelopæus sets us another problem. She seeks the warmth of our fireplaces. Her nest, built of soft mud which would be reduced to pulp by damp, must have a dry shelter. Heat is a necessity to her.

Is it possible that she is a foreigner? Did she come, perhaps, from the shores of Africa, from the land of dates to the land of olives? It would be natural, in that case, that she should find our sunshine not warm enough for her, and should seek the artificial warmth of the fireside. This would explain her habits, so unlike those of the other Wasps, by all of whom mankind is avoided.

What was her life before she became our guest? Where did she lodge before there were any houses? Where did she shelter her grubs before chimneys were thought of?

Perhaps, when the early inhabitants of the hills near Sérignan were making weapons out of flints, scraping goatskins for clothes, and building huts of mud and branches, those huts were already frequented by the Pelopæus. Perhaps she built her nest in some bulging pot, shaped out of clay by the thumbs of our ancestors; or in the folds of the garments, the skins of the Wolf and the Bear. When she made her home on the rough walls of branches and clay, did she choose the nearest spot, I wonder, to the hole in the roof by which the smoke was let out? Though not equal to our chimneys it may have served at a pinch.

If the Pelopæus really lived here with the earliest human inhabitants, what improvements she has seen! She too must have profited greatly by civilisation: she has turned man's increasing comfort into her own. When the dwelling with a roof and a ceiling was planned, and the chimney with a flue was invented, we can imagine the chilly creature saying to herself:

"How pleasant this is! Let us pitch our tent here."

But we will go back further still. Before huts existed, before the niche in the rut, before man himself had appeared, where did the Pelopæus build? The question does not stand alone. Where did the Swallow and the Sparrow build before there were windows and chimneys to build in?

Since the Swallow, the Sparrow, and the Wasp existed before man, their industry cannot be dependent on the works of man. Each of them must have had an art of building in the time when man was not here.

For thirty years and more I asked myself where the Pelopæus lived in those times. Outside our houses I could find no trace of her nests. At last chance, which favours the persevering, came to my help.

The Sérignan quarries are full of broken stones, of refuse that has been piled there in the course of centuries. Here the Fieldmouse crunches his olive-stones and acorns, or now and then a Snail. The empty Snail-shells lie here and there beneath a stone, and within them different Bees and Wasps build their cells. In searching for these treasures I found, three times, the nest of a Pelopæus among the broken stones.

These three nests were exactly the same as those found in our houses. The material was mud, as always; the protective covering was the same mud. The dangers of the site had suggested no improvements to the builder. We see, then, that sometimes, but very rarely, the Pelopæus builds in stoneheaps and under flat blocks of stone that do not touch the ground. It was in such places as these that she must have made her nest before she invaded our houses.

The three nests, however, were in a piteous state. The damp and exposure had ruined them, and the cocoons were in pieces. Unprotected by their earthen cover the grubs had perished— eaten by a Fieldmouse or another.

The sight of these ruins made me wonder if my neighbourhood were really a suitable place for the Pelopæus to build her nest out of doors. It is plain that the mother Wasp dislikes doing so, and is hardly ever driven to such a desperate measure. And if the climate makes it impossible for her to practise the industry of her forefathers successfully, I think we may conclude that she is a foreigner. Surely she comes from a hotter and drier climate, where there is little rain and no snow.

I believe the Pelopæus is of African origin. Far back in the past she came to us through Spain and Italy, and she hardly ever goes further north than the olive-trees. She is an African who has become a naturalised Provençal. In Africa she is said often to nest under stones, but in the Malay Archipelago we hear of her kinswoman in houses. From one end of the world to the other she has the same tastes—Spiders, mud cells, and the shelter of a man's roof. If I were in the Malay Archipelago I should turn over the stone-heaps, and should most likely discover a nest in the original position, under a flat stone.

CHAPTER VII

The Psyches

I

A Well-Dressed Caterpillar

In the springtime, those who have eyes to see may find a surprise on old walls and dusty roads. Certain tiny faggots, for no apparent reason, set themselves in motion and make their way along by sudden jerks. The lifeless comes to life: the immovable moves. This is indeed amazing. If we look closer, however, we shall solve the riddle.

Enclosed within the moving bundle is a fair-sized Caterpillar, prettily striped with black and white. He is seeking for food, and perhaps for some spot where he can turn into a Moth. He hurries along timidly, dressed in a queer garment of twigs, which completely covers the whole of him except his head and the front part of his body, with its six short legs. At the least alarm he disappears entirely into his case, and does not budge again. This is the secret of the walking bundle of sticks. It is a Faggot Caterpillar, belonging to the group known as the Psyches.

To protect himself from the weather the chilly, bare-skinned Psyche builds himself a portable shelter, a travelling cottage which the owner never leaves until he becomes a Moth. It is, indeed, something better than a hut on wheels, with a thatched roof to it: it is more like a hermit's frock, made of an unusual kind of material. In the valley of the Danube the peasant wears a goatskin cloak fastened with a belt of rushes. The Psyche wears even rougher raiment than this: he makes himself a suit of clothes out of sticks. And since this would be a regular hairshirt to a skin so delicate as his, he puts in a thick lining of silk.

In April, on the walls of my chief workshop—my stony *harmas* with its wealth of insect life—I find the Psyche who will supply me with my most detailed information. He is in the torpid state which shows he will soon become a Moth. It is a good opportunity for examining his bundle of sticks, or case.

It is a fairly regular object, shaped like a spindle, and about an inch and a half long. The pieces that compose it are fixed in front and free at the back. They are arranged anyhow, and would form rather a poor shelter against the sun and rain if the hermit had no other protection than this.

At the first glance it appears like thatch; but thatch is not an exact description of it, for grain-stems are rarely found in it. The chief materials are remnants of very small stalks, light, soft, and rich in pith; next in order come bits of grass-leaves, scaly twigs from the cypress-tree, and all sorts of little sticks; and lastly, if the favourite pieces run short, fragments of dry leaves.

In short the Caterpillar, while preferring pithy pieces, will use anything he comes across, provided it be light, very dry, softened by long exposure, and of the right size. All his materials are used just as they are, without any alterations or sawings to make them the proper length. He does not cut the laths that form his roof; he gathers them as he finds them. His work is limited to fixing them at the fore-end.

In order to lend itself to the movements of the travelling Caterpillar, and particularly to enable the head and legs to move freely while a new piece is being fixed in position, the front part of this case or sheath must be made in a special way. Here a casing of sticks is no longer suitable, for their length and stiffness would hamper the workman and even make his work impossible. What is required here is a flexible neck, able to move in all directions. The collection of stakes, therefore, ends suddenly at some distance from the fore-part, and is there replaced by a collar where the silk lining is merely hardened with very tiny particles of wood, which strengthen the material without making it less flexible. This collar, which allows of free movement, is so important that all the Psyches use it, however greatly the rest of their work may differ. All carry, in front of the bundle of sticks, a yielding neck, soft to the touch, formed inside of a web of pure silk and coated outside with a velvety sawdust, which the Caterpillar obtains by crushing up any sort of dry straw.

The same kind of velvet, but dull and faded—apparently through age—finishes the sheath at the back, in the form of a rather long projection, open at the end.

When I remove the outside of the straw casing, shredding it piece by piece, I find a varying number of laths, or tiny sticks. I have counted as many as eighty, and more. Underneath it I find, from one end of the Caterpillar to the other, the same kind of inner sheath that was formerly visible at the front and back only. This inner sheath is composed everywhere of very strong silk, which resists without breaking when pulled by the fingers. It is a smooth tissue, beautifully white inside, drab and wrinkled outside, where it bristles with a crust of woody particles.

Later on we shall see how the Caterpillar makes himself this complicated garment, formed of three layers, one placed upon the other in a definite order. First comes the extremely fine satin which is in direct contact with the skin; next, the mixed stuff dusted with woody matter, which saves the silk and gives strength to the work; and lastly the outer casing of overlapping sticks.

Although all the Psyches wear this threefold garment, the different species make distinct variations in the outer case. There is one kind, for instance, whom I am apt to meet towards the end of June, hurrying across some dusty path near the houses. His case surpasses that of the first species, both in size and in regularity of arrangement. It forms a thick coverlet of many pieces, in which I recognise fragments of hollow stalks, bits of fine straw, and perhaps blades of grass. In front there is never any flounce of dead leaves, a troublesome piece of finery which is pretty frequent, though not always used, in the costume of the first species I described. At the back there is no long projection beyond the outer covering. Save for the indispensable collar at the neck, the whole Caterpillar is cased in sticks. There is not much variety about the thing, but, when all is said, there is a certain beauty in its stern faultlessness.

There is a smaller and more simply dressed Psyche who is very common at the end of winter on the walls, as well as in the bark of gnarled old trees, whether olive-trees or elms, or indeed almost any other. His case, a modest little bundle, is hardly more than two-fifths of an inch in length. A dozen rotten straws, picked up at random and fixed close to one another in a parallel direction, represent, with the silk sheath, his whole outlay on dress.

It would be difficult to clothe oneself more economically.

II

A Devoted Mother

If I gather a number of little Psyches in April and place them in a wire bell-jar, I can find out more about them. Most of them are in the chrysalis state, waiting to be turned into Moths, but a few are still active and clamber to the top of the wire trellis. There they fix themselves by means of a little silk cushion, and both they and I must wait for weeks before anything further happens.

At the end of June the male Psyche comes out of his case, no longer a Caterpillar, but a Moth. The case, or bundle of sticks, you will remember, had two openings, one in front and one at the back. The front one, which is the more regular and carefully made, is permanently closed by being fastened to the support on which the chrysalis is fixed; so the Moth, when he is hatched, is obliged to come out by the opening at the back. The Caterpillar turns round inside the case before he changes into a Moth.

Though they wear but a simple pearl-grey dress and have insignificant wings, hardly larger than those of a Common Fly, these little male Moths are graceful enough. They have handsome feathery plumes for antennæ, and their wings are edged with delicate fringes. For the appearance of the female Psyche, however, little can be said.

Some days later than the others she comes out of the sheath, and shows herself in all her wretchedness. Call that little fright a Moth! One cannot easily get used to the idea of so miserable a sight: as a Caterpillar she was no worse to look at. There are no wings, none at all; there is no silky fur either. At the tip of her round, tufty body she wears a crown of dirty-white velvet; on each segment, in the middle of the back, is a large, rectangular, dark patch—her sole attempts at ornament. The mother Psyche renounces all the beauty which her name of Moth seems to promise.

As she leaves her chrysalid sheath she lays her eggs within it, thus bequeathing the maternal cottage (or the maternal garment, if you will) to her heirs. As she lays a great many eggs the affair takes some thirty hours. When the laying is finished she closes the door and makes everything safe against invasion. For this purpose some kind of wadding is required. The fond mother makes use of the only ornament which, in her extreme poverty, she possesses. She wedges the door with the coronet of velvet which she carries at the tip of her body.

Finally she does even more than this. She makes a rampart of her body itself. With a convulsive movement she dies on the threshold of her recent home, her cast chrysalid skin, and there her remains dry up. Even after death she stays at her post.

If the outer case be now opened it will be found to contain the chrysalid wrapper, uninjured except for the opening in front, by which the Psyche came out. The male Moth, when obliged to make his way through the narrow pass, would find his wings and his plumes very cumbersome articles. For this reason he makes a start for the door while he is still in the chrysalis state, and comes half-way out. Then, as he bursts his amber-coloured tunic, he finds, right in front of him, an open space where flight is possible.

But the mother Moth, being unprovided with wings and plumes, is not compelled to take any such precautions. Her cylinder-like form is bare, and differs very little from that of the Caterpillar. It allows her to crawl, to slip into the narrow passage, and to come forth without difficulty. So she leaves her cast skin behind her, right at the back of the case, well covered by the thatched roof.

And this is an act of prudence, showing her deep concern for the fate of her eggs. They are, in fact, packed as though in a barrel, in the parchment-like bag formed by the cast skin. The Moth has methodically gone on laying eggs in that receptacle till it is full. Not satisfied with bequeathing her house and her velvet coronet to her offspring, as the last act of her life she leaves them her skin.

Wishing to observe the course of events at my ease I once took one of these chrysalid bags, stuffed with eggs, from its outer casing of sticks, and placed it by itself, beside its case, in a glass tube. In the first week of July I suddenly found myself in possession of a large family. The hatching took place so quickly that the new-born Caterpillars, about forty in number, had already clothed themselves in my absence.

They wore a garment like a sort of Persian head-dress, in dazzling white plush. Or, to be more commonplace, a white cotton night-cap without a tassel. Strange to say, however, instead of wearing their caps on their heads, they wore them standing up from their hind-quarters, almost perpendicularly. They roamed about gaily inside the tube, which was a spacious dwelling for such mites. I was quite determined to find out with what materials and in what manner the first outlines of the cap were woven.

Fortunately the chrysalid bag was far from being empty. I found within the rumpled wrapper a second family as numerous as those already out of the case. Altogether there must have been five or six dozen eggs. I transferred to another place the little Caterpillars who were already dressed, keeping only the naked new-comers in the tube. They had bright red heads; the rest of their bodies was dirty-white; and they measured hardly a twenty-fifth of an inch in length.

I had not long to wait. The next day, little by little, singly or in groups, the little laggards left the chrysalid bag. They came out without breaking that frail object, through the opening in front made by their mother. Not one of them used it as a dress-material, though it had the delicacy and amber colouring of an onion-skin; nor did any of them make use of a certain fine quilting that lines the inside of the bag and forms an exquisitely soft bed for the eggs. One would have thought this downy stuff would make an excellent blanket for the chilly creatures, but not a single one used it. There would not be enough to go round.

They all went straight to the coarse outer casing of sticks, which I had left in contact with the chrysalid skin containing the eggs. The matter was urgent, they evidently felt. Before making your entrance into the world and going a-hunting, you must first be clad. All therefore, with equal fury, attacked the old sheath and hastily dressed themselves in their mother's old clothes.

Some turned their attention to bits that happened to be opened lengthwise, scraping the soft white inner layer; others, greatly daring, penetrated into the tunnel of a hollow stalk and collected their materials in the dark. The courage of these was rewarded; they secured first-rate materials and wove garments of dazzling white. There were others who bit deeply into the piece they chose, and made themselves a motley covering, in which the snowy whiteness was marred by darker particles.

The tools the little Caterpillars use for this purpose are their mandibles, which are shaped like wide shears and have five strong teeth apiece. The two blades fit into each other, and form an instrument capable of seizing and slicing any fibre, however small. Under the microscope it is seen to be a wonderful specimen of mechanical precision and power. If the Sheep had a similar tool in proportion to her size, she could browse on the stems of trees instead of the grass.

It is very instructive to watch these Psyche-grubs toiling to make themselves a cotton night-cap. There are numbers of things to remark, both in the finish of the work and the skill of the methods they employ. They are so tiny that while I observe them through my magnifying glass I must be careful not to breathe, lest I should overturn them or puff them away. Yet this speck is expert in the art of blanket-making. An orphan, born but a moment ago, it knows how to cut itself a garment out of its mother's old clothes. Of its methods I will tell you more presently, but first I must say another word with regard to its dead mother.

I have spoken of the downy quilting that covers the inside of the chrysalid bag. It is like a bed of eider-down, on which the little Caterpillars rest for a while after leaving the egg. Warmly nestling in this soft rug they prepare themselves for their plunge into the outer world of work.

The Eider robs herself of her down to make a luxurious bed for her brood; the mother Rabbit shears from her own body the softest part of her fur to provide a mattress for her new-born family. And the same thing is done by the Psyche.

The mass of soft wadding that makes a warm coverlet for the baby Caterpillar is a material of incomparable delicacy. Through the microscope it can be recognised as the scaly dust, the intensely fine down in which every Moth is clad. To give a snug shelter to the little grubs who will soon be swarming in the case, to provide them with a refuge in which they can play about and gather strength before entering the wide world, the Psyche strips herself of her fur like the mother Rabbit.

This may possibly be done mechanically; it may be the unintentional effect of rubbing repeatedly against the low-roofed walls; but there is nothing to tell us so. Even the humblest mother has her foresight. It is quite likely that the hairy Moth twists about, and goes to and fro in the narrow passage, in order to get rid of her fleece and prepare bedding for her family.

I have read in books that the young Psyches begin life by eating up their mother. I have seen nothing of the sort, and I do not even understand how the idea arose. Indeed, she has given up so much for her family that there is nothing left of her but some thin, dry strips—not enough to provide a meal for so numerous a brood. No, my little Psyches, you do not eat your mother. In vain do I watch you: never, either to clothe or to feed himself, does any one of you lay a tooth upon the remains of the deceased.

III

A Clever Tailor

I will now describe in greater detail the dressing of the grubs.

The hatching of the eggs takes place in the first fortnight of July. The head and upper part of the little grubs are of a glossy black, the next two segments are brownish, and the rest of the body is a pale amber. They are sharp, lively little creatures, who run about with short, quick steps.

For a time, after they are out of the bag where they are hatched, they remain in the heap of fluff that was stripped from their mother. Here there is more room, and more comfort too, than in the bag whence they came; and while some take a rest, others bustle about and exercise themselves in walking. They are all picking up strength before leaving the outer case.

They do not stay long amid this luxury. Gradually, as they gain vigour, they come out and spread over the surface of the case. Work begins at once, a very urgent work—that of dressing themselves. By and by they will think of food: at present nothing is of any importance but clothes.

Montaigne, when putting on a cloak which his father had worn before him, used to say, "I dress myself in my father." Well, the young Psyches in the same way dress themselves in their mother. (In the *same way*, it must be remembered; not in her skin, but in her clothes.) From the outer case of sticks, which I have sometimes described as a house and sometimes as a garment, they scrape the material to make themselves a frock. The stuff they use is the pith of the little stalks, especially of the pieces that are split lengthwise, because the contents are more easily taken from these.

The manner of beginning the garment is worth noting. The tiny creature employs a method as ingenious as any that we could hope to discover. The wadding is collected in pellets of infinitesimal size. How are these little pellets to be fixed and joined together? The manufacturer needs a support, a base; and this support cannot be obtained on the Caterpillar's own body. The difficulty is overcome very cleverly. The pellets are gathered together, and by degrees fastened to one another with threads of silk—for the Caterpillar, as you know, can spin silk from his own body as the Spider spins her web. In this way a sort of garland is formed, with the pellets or particles swinging in a row from the same rope. When it is long enough this garland is passed round the waist of the little creature, in such a way as to leave its six legs free. Then it ties the ends together with a bit of silk, so that it forms a girdle round the grub's body.

This girdle is the starting-point and support of the whole work. To lengthen it, and enlarge it into a complete garment, the grub has only to fix to it the scraps of pith which the mandibles never cease tearing from the case. These scraps or pellets are sometimes placed at the top, sometimes at the bottom or side, but they are always fixed at the fore-edge. No device could be better contrived than this garland, first laid out flat and then buckled like a belt round the body.

Once this start is made the weaving goes on well. Gradually the girdle grows into a scarf, a waistcoat, a short jacket, and lastly a sack, and in a few hours it is complete—a conical hood or cloak of magnificent whiteness.

Thanks to his mother's care the little grub is spared the perils of roaming about in a state of nakedness. If she did not place her family in her old case they might have great difficulty in clothing themselves, for straws and stalks rich in pith are not found everywhere. And yet, unless they died of exposure, it appears that sooner or later they would find some kind of garment, since they seem ready to use any material that comes to hand. I have made many experiments with new-born grubs in a glass tube.

From the stalks of a sort of dandelion they scraped, without the least hesitation, a superb white pith, and made it into a delicious white cloak, much finer than any they would have obtained from the remains of their mother's clothes. An even better garment was woven from some pith taken from the kitchen-broom. This time the work glittered with little sparks, like specks of crystal or grains of sugar. It was my manufacturers' masterpiece.

The next material I offered them was a piece of blotting-paper. Here again my grubs did not hesitate: they lustily scraped the surface and made themselves a paper coat. Indeed, they were so much pleased with this that when I gave them their native case they scorned it, preferring the blotting-paper.

To others I gave nothing at all. Not to be baffled, however, they hastened to scrape the cork of the tube and break it into atoms. Out of these they made themselves a frock of cork-grains, as faultless as though they and their ancestors had always made use of this material. The novelty of the stuff, which perhaps no Caterpillar had ever used before, made no difference in the cut of the garment.

Finding them ready to accept any vegetable matter that was dry and light, I next tried them with animal and mineral substances. I cut a strip from the wing of a Great Peacock Moth, and placed two little naked Caterpillars upon it. For a long time they both hesitated. Then one of them resolved to use the strange carpet. Before the day was over he had clothed himself in grey velvet made of the Great Peacock's scales.

I next took some soft, flaky stones, such as will break at the merest touch into atoms nearly as fine as the dust on a Butterfly's wing. On a bed of this powdery stuff, which glittered like steel filings, I placed four Caterpillars in need of clothes. One, and one alone, decided to dress himself. His metallic garment, from which the light drew flashes of every colour of the rainbow, was very rich and sumptuous, but mightily heavy and cumbrous. Walking became laborious under that load of metal. Even so must a Byzantine Emperor have walked at ceremonies of State.

In cases of necessity, then, the young Caterpillar does not shrink from acts of sheer madness. So urgent is his need to clothe himself that he will weave mineral matter rather than go naked. Food means less to him than clothes. If I make him fast for a couple of days, and then, having robbed him of his garment, place him on his favourite food, a leaf of very hairy hawk-weed, he will make himself a new coat before satisfying his hunger.

This devotion to dress is due, not to any special sensitiveness to cold, but to the young Caterpillar's foresight. Other Caterpillars take shelter among the leaves, in underground cells, or in the cracked bark of trees, but the Psyche spends his winter exposed to the weather. He therefore prepares himself, from his birth, for the perils of the cold season.

As soon as he is threatened with the rains of autumn he begins to work upon his outer case. It is very rough at first. Straws of uneven length and bits of dry leaves are fastened, with no attempt at order, behind the neck of the sack or undergarment, which must remain flexible so as to allow the Caterpillar to bend freely in every direction. These untidy first logs of the outer case will not interfere with the final regularity of the building: they will be pushed back and driven out as the sack grows longer in front.

After a time the pieces are longer and more carefully chosen, and are all laid on lengthwise. The placing of a straw is done with surprising speed and skill. The Caterpillar turns it round and round between his legs, and then, gripping it in his mandibles, removes a few morsels from one end, and immediately fixes them to the end of the sack. He probably does this in order that the silk may obtain a firmer hold, as a plumber gives a touch of the file to a point that is to be soldered.

Then, by sheer strength of jaw, he lifts and brandishes his straw in the air before laying it on his back. At once the spinneret sets to work and fixes it in place. Without any groping about or correcting, the thing is done. By the time the cold weather arrives the warm case is complete.

But the silky felt of the interior is never thick enough to please the Caterpillar. When spring comes he spends all his spare time in improving his quilt, in making it ever thicker and softer. Even if I take off his outer case he refuses to rebuild it: he persists in adding new layers to the lining, even when there is nothing to be lined. The sack is lamentably flabby; it sags and rumples. He has no protection nor shelter. No matter. The hour for carpentry has passed. The hour has come for upholstering; and he upholsters obstinately, padding a house—or lining a garment—that no longer exists. He will perish miserably, cut up by the Ants, as the result of his too-rigid instinct.

CHAPTER VIII

The Self-Denial of the Spanish Copris

You remember, I hope, the Sacred Beetle, who spends her time in making balls, both to serve as food and also to be the foundation of her pear-shaped nest. I pointed out the advantages of this shape for the young Beetles, since the globe is the best form that could be invented to keep their provisions from becoming dry and hard.

After watching this Beetle at work for a long time I began to wonder if I had not perhaps been mistaken in admiring her instinct so greatly. Was it really care for her grubs, I asked myself, that taught her to provide them with the tenderest and most suitable food? It is the trade of the Sacred Beetle to make balls. Is it wonderful that she should continue her ball-making underground? A creature built with long curved legs, very useful for rolling balls across the fields, will go on with her favourite occupation wherever she may be, without regard to her grubs. Perhaps the shape of the pear is mere chance.

To settle this question satisfactorily in my own mind I should need to be shown a Scavenger Beetle who was utterly unfamiliar with the ball-making business in everyday life, and who yet, when laying-time was at hand, made an abrupt change in her habits and stored her provisions in the form of a round lump. That would show me that it was not merely custom, but care for her grubs, that made her choose the globular shape for her nest.

Now in my neighbourhood there is a Beetle of this very kind. She is one of the handsomest and largest, though not so imposing as the Sacred Beetle. Her name is the Spanish Copris, and she is remarkable for the sharp slope of her chest and the size of the horn surmounting her head.

Being round and squat, the Spanish Copris is certainly incapable of such gymnastics as are performed by the Sacred Beetle. Her legs, which are insignificant in length, and which she folds under her body at the slightest alarm, are not in the least like the stilts of the pill-rollers. Their stunted form and their lack of flexibility are enough in themselves to tell us that their owner would not care to roam about burdened with a rolling ball.

The Copris, indeed, is not of an active nature. Once she has found her provisions, at night or in the evening twilight, she begins to dig a burrow on the spot. It is a rough cavern, large enough to hold an apple. Here is introduced, bit by bit, the stuff that is just overhead, or at any rate lying on the threshold of the cave. An enormous supply of food is stored in a shapeless mass, plain evidence of the insect's gluttony. As long as the hoard lasts the Copris remains underground. When the larder is empty the insect searches out a fresh supply of food, and scoops out another burrow.

For the time being the Copris is merely a scavenger, a gatherer of manure. She is evidently quite ignorant, at present, of the art of kneading and modelling a round loaf. Besides, her short clumsy legs seem utterly unsuited for any such art.

In May or June, however, comes laying-time. The insect becomes very particular about choosing the softest materials for her family's food. Having found what pleases her, she buries it on the spot, carrying it down by armfuls, bit by bit. There is no travelling, no carting, no preparation. I observe, too, that the burrow is larger and better built than the temporary abodes in which the Copris takes her own meals.

Finding it difficult to observe the insect closely in its wild state, I resolved to place it in my insect-house, and there watch it at my ease.

The poor creature was at first a little nervous in captivity, and when she had made her burrow was very cautious about entering it. By degrees, however, she was reassured, and in a single night she stored a supply of the food I had provided for her.

Before a week was out I dug up the soil in my insect-house,

and brought to light the burrow I had seen her storing with provisions. It was a spacious hall, with an irregular roof and an
almost level floor. In a corner was a round hole leading to a
slanting gallery, which ran up to the surface of the soil. The walls
of this dwelling, which was hollowed out of fresh earth, had
been carefully compressed, and were strong enough to resist the
earthquake caused by my experiments. It was easy to see that
the insect had put forth all her skill, all her digging-powers, in
the making of this permanent home, whereas her own dining-
room had been a mere cave, with walls that were none too safe.

I suspect she is helped, in the building of this architectural
masterpiece, by her mate: at least I often see him with her in the
burrows. I also believe that he lends his partner a hand with the
collecting and storing of the provisions. It is a quicker job when
there are two to work. But once the home is well stocked he
retires: he makes his way back to the surface and settles down
elsewhere. His part in the family mansion is ended.

Now what do I find in this mansion, into which I have seen so
many tiny loads of provisions lowered? A mass of small pieces,
heaped together anyhow? Not a bit of it. I always find a simple
lump, a huge mass which fills the dwelling except for a narrow
passage.

This lump has no fixed shape. I come across some that are like
a Turkey's egg in form and size; some the shape of a common
onion; I find some that are almost round, and remind me of a
Dutch cheese; I see some that are circular, with a slight swelling
on the upper surface. In every case the surface is smooth and
nicely curved.

There is no mistaking what has happened. The mother has
collected and kneaded into one lump the numerous fragments
brought down one after the other. Out of all those particles she
has made a single lump, by mashing them, working them
together, and treading on them. Time after time I have seen her
on top of the colossal loaf which is so much larger than the ball
of the Sacred Beetle—a mere pill in comparison. She strolls
about on the convex surface, which sometimes measures as
much as four inches across; she pats the mass, and makes it firm
and level. I only catch a sight of the curious scene, for the

moment she sees me she slips down the curved slope and hides away.

With the help of a row of glass jars, all enclosed in opaque sheaths of cardboard, I can find out a good many interesting things. In the first place I have found that the big loaf does not owe its curve—which is always regular, no matter how much the slope may vary—to any rolling process. Indeed I already knew that so large a mess could not have been rolled into a hole that it nearly fills. Besides, the strength of the insect would be unequal to moving so great a load.

Every time I go to the jar the evidence is the same. I always see the mother Beetle twisted on top of the lump, feeling here and feeling there, giving little taps, and making the thing smooth. Never do I catch her looking as if she wanted to turn the block. It is clear as daylight that rolling has nothing to do with the matter.

At last it is ready. The baker divides his lump of dough into smaller lumps, each of which will become a loaf. The Copris does the same thing. By making a circular cut with the sharp edge of her forehead, and at the same time using the saw of her fore-legs, she detaches from the mass a piece of the size she requires. In giving this stroke she has no hesitation: there are no after-touches, adding a bit here and taking off a bit there. Straight away, with one sharp, decisive cut, she obtains the proper-sized lump.

Next comes the question of shaping it. Clasping it as best she can in her short arms, so little adapted, one would think, for work of this kind, the Copris rounds her lump of food by pressure, and pressure only. Solemnly she moves about on the still shapeless mass, climbs up, climbs down, turns to right and left, above and below, touching and re-touching with unvarying patience. Finally, after twenty-four hours of this work, the piece that was all corners has become a perfect sphere, the size of a plum. There in her cramped studio, with scarcely room to move, the podgy artist has completed her work without once shaking it on its base: by dint of time and patience she has obtained the exact sphere which her clumsy tools and her confined space seemed to render impossible.

For a long time she continues to polish up the globe with affectionate touches of her foot, but at last she is satisfied. She climbs to the top, and by simple pressure hollows out a shallow cavity. In this basin she lays an egg.

Then, with extreme caution and delicacy, she brings together the sides of the basin so as to cover the egg, and carefully scrapes the sides towards the top, which begins to taper a little and length-en out. In the end the ball has become ovoid, or egg-shaped.

The insect next helps herself to a second piece of the cut loaf, which she treats in the same way. The remainder serves for a third ovoid, or even a fourth. The Sacred Beetle, you remember, made a single pear-shaped nest in a way that was familiar to her, and then left her egg underground while she engaged in fresh enterprises. The Copris behaves very differently.

Her burrow is almost filled by three or four ovoid nests, standing one against the other, with the pointed end upwards. After her long fast one would expect her to go away, like the Sacred Beetle, in search of food. On the contrary, however, she stays where she is. And yet she has eaten nothing since she came underground, for she has taken good care not to touch the food prepared for her family. She will go hungry rather than let her grubs suffer.

Her object in staying is to mount guard over the cradles. The pear of the Sacred Beetle suffers from the mother's desertion. It soon shows cracks, and becomes scaly and swollen. After a time it loses its shape. But the nest of the Copris remains perfect, owing to the mother's care. She goes from one to the other, feels them, listens to them, and touches them up at points where my eye can detect no flaw. Her clumsy horn-shod foot is more sen-sitive in the darkness than my sight in broad daylight: she feels the least threatening of a crack and attends to it at once, lest the air should enter and dry up her eggs. She slips in and out of the narrow spaces between the cradles, inspecting them with the utmost care. If I disturb her she sometimes rubs the tip of her body against the edge of her wing-cases, making a soft rustling sound, like a murmur of complaint. In this way, caring industri-ously for her cradles, and sometimes snatching a brief sleep beside them, the mother waits.

The Copris enjoys in her underground home a rare privilege for an insect: the pleasure of knowing her family. She hears her grubs scratching at the shell to obtain their liberty; she is present at the bursting of the nest which she has made so carefully. And when the little captive, stiffening his legs and humping his back, tries to split the ceiling that presses down on him, it is quite possible that the mother comes to his assistance by making an assault on the nest from the outside. Being fitted by instinct for repairing and building, why should she not also be fitted for demolishing? However, I will make no assertions, for I have been unable to see.

Now it is possible to say that the mother Copris, being imprisoned in an enclosure from which she cannot escape, stays in the midst of her nest because she has no choice in the matter. Yet, if this were so, would she trouble about her work of polishing and constant inspection? These cares evidently are natural to her: they form part of her habits. If she were anxious to regain her liberty, she would surely roam restlessly round the enclosure, whereas I always see her very quiet and absorbed.

To make certain, I have inspected my glass jars at different times. She could go lower down in the sand and hide anywhere she pleased, if rest were what she wanted; she could climb outside and sit down to fresh food, if refreshment became necessary. Neither the prospect of rest in a deeper cave nor the thought of the sun and of food makes her leave her family. Until the last of them has burst his shell she sticks to her post. I always find her beside her cradles.

For four months she is without food of any kind. She was no better than a glutton at first, when there was no family to consider, but now she becomes self-denying to the point of prolonged fasting. The Hen sitting on her eggs forgets to eat for some weeks; the watchful Copris mother forgets food for a third part of the year.

The summer is over. The rains so greatly desired by man and beast have come at last, soaking the ground to some depth. After the torrid and dusty days of our Provençal summer, when life is in suspense, we have the coolness that revives it. The heath puts out its first pink bells; the autumnal squill lifts its little spike of

lilac flowers; the strawberry-tree's coral bells begin to soften; the
Sacred Beetle and the Copris burst their shells, and come to the
surface in time to enjoy the last fine weather of the year.

The newly released Copris family, accompanied by their
mother, gradually emerge from underground. There are three
or four of them, five at most. The sons are easily recognised by
the greater length of their horns; but there is nothing to distinguish the daughters from the mother. For that matter, the same
confusion exists among themselves. An abrupt change has taken
place. The mother whose devotion was lately so remarkable is
now utterly indifferent to the welfare of her family. Hence-
forward each looks after his own home and his own interests.
They no longer have anything to do with one another.

The present indifference of the mother Beetle must not make
us forget the wonderful care she has lavished for four months on
end. Except among the Bees, Wasps, and Ants, who spoon-feed
their young and bring them up with every attention to their
health, I know of no other such case of maternal self-denial.
Alone and unaided she provides each of her children with a cake
of food, whose crust she constantly repairs, so that it becomes
the safest of cradles. So intense is her affection that she loses all
desire and need of food. In the darkness of the burrow she
watches over her brood for four months, attending to the wants
of the egg, the grub, the undeveloped Beetle, and the full-
grown insect. She does not return to the glad outer life till all
her family are free. Thus we see one of the most brilliant examples of maternal instinct in a humble scavenger of the fields.
The Spirit breatheth where He will.

CHAPTER IX

Two Strange Grasshoppers

I

The Empusa

The sea, where life first appeared, still preserves in its depths many of those curious shapes which were the earliest specimens of the animal kingdom. But the land has almost entirely lost the strange forms of other days. The few that remain are mostly insects. One of these is the Praying Mantis, whose remarkable shape and habits I have already described to you. Another is the Empusa.

This insect, in its undeveloped or larval state, is certainly the strangest creature in all Provence: a slim, swaying thing of so fantastic an appearance that unaccustomed fingers dare not lay hold of it. The children of my neighbourhood are so much impressed by its startling shape that they call it "the Devilkin." They imagine it to be in some way connected with witchcraft. One comes across it, though never in great numbers, in the spring up to May; in autumn; and sometimes in winter if the sun be strong. The tough grasses of the waste-lands, the stunted bushes which catch the sunshine and are sheltered from the wind by a few heaps of stones, are the chilly Empusa's favourite dwelling.

I will tell you, as well as I can, what she looks like. The tail-end of her body is always twisted and curved up over her back so as to form a crook, and the lower surface of her body (that is to say, of course, the upper surface of the crook) is covered with pointed, leaf-shaped scales, arranged in three rows. The crook is propped on four long, thin legs, like stilts; and on each of these legs, at the point where the thigh joins the shin, is a curved, projecting blade not unlike that of a cleaver.

In front of this crook on stilts, this four-legged stool, there rises suddenly—very long and almost perpendicular—the stiff corselet or bust. It is round and slender as a straw, and at the end of it is the hunting-trap, copied from that of the Mantis. This consists of a harpoon sharper than a needle, and a cruel vice with jaws toothed like a saw. The jaw, or blade formed by the upper arm, is hollowed into a groove and carries five long spikes on each side, with smaller indentations in between. The jaw formed by the fore-arm is grooved in the same way, but the teeth are finer, closer, and more regular. When at rest, the saw of the fore-arm fits into the groove of the upper arm. If the machine were only larger it would be a fearful instrument of torture.

The head is in keeping with this arsenal. What a queer head it is! A pointed face, with curled moustaches; large goggle eyes; between them the blade of a dirk; and on the forehead a mad, unheard-of thing—a sort of tall mitre, an extravagant head-dress that juts forward, spreading right and left into peaked wings. What does the Devilkin want with that monstrous pointed cap, as magnificent as any ever worn by astrologer of old? The use of it will appear presently.

The creature's colouring at this time is commonplace—chiefly grey. As it develops it becomes faintly striped with pale green, white, and pink.

If you come across this fantastic object in the bramble-bushes, it sways upon its four stilts, it wags its head at you knowingly, it twists its mitre round and peers over its shoulder. You seem to see mischief in its pointed face. But if you try to take hold of it this threatening attitude disappears at once; the raised corselet is lowered, and the creature makes off with mighty strides, helping itself along with its weapons, with which it clutches the twigs. If you have a practiced eye, however, the Empusa is easily caught, and penned in a cage of wire-gauze.

At first I was uncertain how to feed them. My Devilkins were very little, a month or two old at most. I gave them Locusts suited to their size, the smallest I could find. They not only refused them, but were afraid of them. Any thoughtless Locust that meekly approached an Empusa met with a bad reception. The pointed mitre was lowered, and an angry thrust sent the Locust rolling. The wizard's cap, then, is a defensive weapon. As the Ram charges with his forehead, so the Empusa butts with her mitre.

I next offered her a live House-fly, and this time the dinner was accepted at once. The moment the Fly came within reach the watchful Devilkin turned her head, bent her corselet slantwise, harpooned the Fly, and gripped it between her two saws. No Cat could pounce more quickly on a Mouse.

To my surprise I found that the Fly was not only enough for a meal, but enough for the whole day, and often for several days. These fierce-looking insects are extremely abstemious. I was expecting them to be ogres, and found them with the delicate appetites of invalids. After a time even a Midge failed to tempt them, and through the winter months they fasted altogether. When the spring came, however, they were ready to indulge in a small piece of Cabbage Butterfly or Locust; attacking their prey invariably in the neck, like the Mantis.

The young Empusa has one very curious habit when in captivity. In its cage of wire-gauze its attitude is the same from first to last, and a most strange attitude it is. It grips the wire by the claws of its four hind-legs, and hangs motionless, back downwards, with the whole of its body suspended from those four points. If it wishes to move, its harpoons open in front, stretch out, grasp a mesh of the wire, and pull. This process naturally draws the insect along the wire, still upside down. Then the jaws close back against the chest.

And this upside-down position, which seems to us so trying, lasts for no short while. It continues, in my cages, for ten months without a break. The Fly on the ceiling, it is true, adopts the same position; but she has her moments of rest. She flies, she walks in the usual way, she spreads herself flat in the sun. The Empusa, on the other hand, remains in her curious attitude for ten months on end, without a pause. Hanging from the wire netting, back downwards, she hunts, eats, digests, dozes, gets through all the experiences of an insect's life, and finally dies. She clambers up while she is still quite young; she falls down in her old age, a corpse.

This custom is all the more remarkable in that it is practised only in captivity. It is not an instinctive habit of the race; for out of doors the insect, except at rare intervals, stands on the bushes back upwards.

Strange as the performance is, I know of a similar case that is even more peculiar: the attitude of certain Wasps and Bees during the night's rest. A particular Wasp, an Ammophila with red fore-legs, is plentiful in my enclosure towards the end of August, and likes to sleep in one of the lavender borders. At dusk, especially after a stifling day when a storm is brewing, I am sure to find the strange sleeper settled there. Never was a more eccentric attitude chosen for a night's rest. The jaws bite right into the lavender-stem. Its square shape supplies a firmer hold than a round stalk would give. With this one and only prop the Wasp's body juts out stiffly at full length, with legs folded. It forms a right angle with the stalk, so that the whole weight of the insect rests upon the mandibles.

The Ammophila is enabled by its mighty jaws to sleep in this way, extended in space. It takes an animal to think of a thing like that, which upsets all our previous ideas of rest. Should the threatening storm burst and the stalk sway in the wind, the sleeper is not troubled by her swinging hammock; at most, she presses her fore-legs for a moment against the tossing stem. Perhaps the Wasp's jaws, like the Bird's toes, possess the power of gripping more tightly in proportion to the violence of the wind. However that may be, there are several kinds of Wasps and Bees who adopt this strange position,—gripping a stalk with their mandibles, and sleeping with their bodies outstretched and their legs folded back. This state of things makes us wonder what it is that really constitutes rest.

About the middle of May the Empusa is transformed into her full-grown condition. She is even more remarkable in figure and attire than the Praying Mantis. She still keeps some of her youthful eccentricities—the bust, the weapons on her knees, and the three rows of scales on the lower surface of her body. But she is now no longer twisted into a crook, and is comelier to look upon. Large pale-green wings, pink at the shoulder and swift in flight, cover the white and green stripes that ornament the body below. The male Empusa, who is a dandy, adorns himself, like some of the Moths, with feathery antennæ.

When, in the spring, the peasant meets the Empusa, he thinks he sees the common Praying Mantis, who is a daughter of the autumn. They are so much alike that one would expect them to have the same habits. In fact, any one might be tempted, led away by the extraordinary armour, to suspect the Empusa of a mode of life even more atrocious than that of the Mantis. This would be a mistake: for all their war-like aspect the Empusæ are peaceful creatures.

Imprisoned in their wire-gauze bell-jar, either in groups of half a dozen or in separate couples, they at no time lose their placidity. Even in their full-grown state they are very small eaters, and content themselves with a fly or two as their daily ration.

Big eaters are naturally quarrelsome. The Mantis, gorged with Locusts, soon becomes irritated and shows fight. The Empusa, with her frugal meals, is a lover of peace. She indulges in no quarrels with her neighbours, nor does she pretend to be a ghost, with a view to frightening them, after the manner of the Mantis. She never unfurls her wings suddenly nor puffs like a startled Adder. She has never the least inclination for the cannibal banquets at which a sister, after being worsted in a fight, is eaten up. Nor does she, like the Mantis, devour her husband. Such atrocities are here unknown.

The organs of the two insects are the same. These profound moral differences, therefore, are not due to any difference in the bodily form. Possibly they may arise from the difference in food. Simple living, as a matter of fact, softens character, in animals as in men; over-feeding brutalises it. The glutton, gorged with meat and strong drink—a very common cause of savage outbursts—could never be as gentle as the self-denying hermit who lives on bread dipped into a cup of milk. The Mantis is a glutton: the Empusa lives the simple life.

And yet, even when this is granted, one is forced to ask a further question. Why, when the two insects are almost exactly the same in form, and might be expected to have the same needs, should the one have an enormous appetite and the other such temperate ways? They tell us, in their own fashion, what many insects have told us already: that inclinations and habits do not depend entirely upon anatomy. High above the laws that govern matter rise other laws that govern instincts.

II

The White-Faced Decticus

The White-faced Decticus stands at the head of the Grasshopper clan in my district, both as a singer and as an insect of imposing presence. He has a grey body, a pair of powerful mandibles, and a broad ivory face. Without being plentiful, he is neither difficult nor wearisome to hunt. In the height of summer we find him hopping in the long grass, especially at the foot of the sunny rocks where the turpentine-tree takes root.

The Greek word *dectikos* means biting, fond of biting. The Decticus is well named. It is eminently an insect given to biting. Mind your finger if this sturdy Grasshopper gets hold of it: he will rip it till the blood comes. His powerful jaw, of which I have to beware when I handle him, and the large muscles that swell out his cheeks, are evidently intended for cutting up leathery prey.

I find, when the Decticus is imprisoned in my menagerie, that any fresh meat tasting of Locust or Grasshopper suits his needs. The blue-winged Locust is the most frequent victim. As soon as the food is introduced into the cage there is an uproar, especially if the Dectici are hungry. They stamp about, and dart forward clumsily, being hampered by their long shanks. Some of the Locusts are caught at once, but others with desperate bounds rush to the top of the cage, and there hang on out of the reach of the Grasshopper, who is too stout to climb so high. But they have only postponed their fate. Either because they are tired, or because they are tempted by the green stuff below, they will come down, and the Dectici will be after them immediately.

This Grasshopper, though his intellect is dull, possesses the art of scientific killing of which we have seen instances elsewhere. He always spears his prey in the neck, and, to make it helpless as quickly as possible, begins by biting the nerves that enable it to move. It is a very wise method, for the Locust is hard to kill. Even when beheaded he goes on hopping. I have seen some who, though half-eaten, kicked out so desperately that they succeeded in escaping.

With his weakness for Locusts, and also for certain seeds that are harmful to unripe corn, these Grasshoppers might be of some service to agriculture if only there were more of them. But nowadays his assistance in preserving the fruits of the earth is very feeble. His chief interest in our eyes is the fact that he is a memorial of the remotest times. He gives us a vague glimpse of habits now out of use.

It was thanks to the Decticus that I first learnt one or two things about young Grasshoppers.

Instead of packing their eggs in casks of hardened foam, like the Locust and the Mantis, or laying them in a twig like the Cicada, Grasshoppers plant them like seeds in the earth.

The mother Decticus has a tool at the end of her body with which she scrapes out a little hole in the soil. In this hole she lays a certain number of eggs, then loosens the dust round the side of the hole and rams it down with her tool, very much as we should pack the earth in a hole with a stick. In this way she covers up the well, and then sweeps and smooths the ground above it.

She then goes for a little walk in the neighbourhood, by way of recreation. Soon she comes back to the place where she has already laid her eggs, and, very near the original spot, which she recognises quite well, begins the work afresh. If I watch her for an hour I see her go through this whole performance, including the short stroll in the neighbourhood, no less than five times. The points where she lays the eggs are always very close together.

When everything is finished I examine the little pits. The eggs lie singly, without any cell or sheath to protect them. There are about sixty of them altogether, pale lilac-grey in colour, and shaped like a shuttle.

When I began to observe the ways of the Decticus I was anxious to watch the hatching, so at the end of August I gathered plenty of eggs, and placed them in a small glass jar with a layer of sand. Without suffering any apparent change they spent eight months there under cover, sheltered from the frosts, the showers, and the overpowering heat of the sun, which they would be obliged to endure out of doors.

When June came, the eggs in my jar showed no sign of being about to hatch. They were just as I had gathered them nine months before, neither wrinkled nor tarnished, but on the contrary wearing a most healthy look. Yet in June young Dectici are often to be met in the fields, and sometimes even those of larger growth. What was the reason of this delay, I wondered.

Then an idea came to me. The eggs of the Grasshopper are planted like seeds in the earth, where they are exposed, without any protection, to snow and rain. Those in my jar had spent two-thirds of the year in a state of comparative dryness. Since they were sown like seeds, perhaps they needed, to make them hatch, the moisture that seeds require to make them sprout. I resolved to try.

I placed at the bottom of some glass tubes a pinch of backward eggs taken from my collection, and on the top I heaped lightly a layer of fine, damp sand. I closed the tubes with plugs of wet cotton, to keep the air in them constantly moist. Any one seeing my preparations would have supposed me to be a botanist experimenting with seeds.

My hopes were fulfilled. In the warmth and moisture the eggs soon showed signs of hatching. They began to swell, and the bursting of the shell was evidently close at hand. I spent a fortnight in keeping a tedious watch at every hour of the day, for I had to surprise the young Decticus actually leaving the egg, in order to solve a question that had long been in my mind.

The question was this. The Grasshopper is buried, as a rule, about an inch below the surface of the soil. Now the new-born Decticus, hopping awkwardly in the grass at the approach of summer, has, like the full-grown insect, a pair of very long tentacles, as slender as hairs; while he carries behind him two extraordinary legs, two enormous hinged jumping-poles that would be very inconvenient for ordinary walking. I wished to find out how the feeble little creature set to work, with this cumbrous luggage, to make its way to the surface of the earth. By what means could it clear a passage through the rough soil? With its feathery antennæ, which an atom of sand can break, and its immense shanks, which are disjointed by the least effort, this mite is plainly incapable of freeing itself.

As I have already told you, the Cicada and the Praying Mantis, when issuing, the one from his twig, and the other from his nest, wear a protective covering like an overall. It seemed to me that the little Grasshopper, too, must come out through the sand in a simpler, more compact form than he wears when he hops about the lawn on the day after his birth.

Now was I mistaken. The Decticus, like the others, wears an overall for the occasion. The tiny, flesh-white creature is cased in a scabbard which keeps the six legs flattened against the body, stretching backwards, inert. In order to slip more easily through the soil his shanks are tied up beside him; while the antennæ, those other inconvenient appendages, are pressed motionless against the parcel.

The head is very much bent against the chest. With the big black specks that are going to be its eyes, and its inexpressive, rather swollen mask, it suggests a diver's helmet. The neck opens wide at the back, and, with a slow throbbing, by turns swells and sinks. It is by means of this throbbing protrusion through the opening at the back of the head that the new-born insect moves. When the lump is flat, the head pushes back the damp sand a little way and slips into it by digging a tiny pit. Then the swelling is blown out and becomes a knob which sticks firmly in the hole. This supplies the resistance necessary for the grub to draw up its back and push. Thus a step forward is made. Each thrust of the motor-blister helps the little Decticus upon the upward path.

It is pitiful to see this tender creature, still almost colourless, knocking with its swollen neck and ramming the rough soil. With flesh that is not yet hardened it is painfully fighting stone; and fighting it so successfully that in the space of a morning it makes a gallery, either straight or winding, an inch long and as wide as an average straw. In this way the harassed insect reaches the surface.

Before it is altogether freed from the soil the struggler halts for a moment, to recover from the effects of the journey. Then, with renewed strength, it makes a last effort: it swells the pro-trusion at the back of its head as far as it will go, and bursts the sheath that has protected it so far. The creature throws off its overall.

Here, then, is the Decticus in his youthful shape, quite pale still, but darker the next day, and a regular blackamoor com-pared with the full-grown insect. As a prelude to the ivory face of his riper age he wears a narrow white stripe under his hinder thighs.

Little Decticus, hatched before my eyes, life opens for you very harshly! Many of your relatives must die of exhaustion before winning their freedom. In my tubes I see numbers who, being stopped by a grain of sand, give up the struggle half-way and become furred with a sort of silky fluff. Mildew soon absorbs their poor little remains. And when carried out without my help, their journey to the surface must be even more dan-gerous, for the soil out of doors is coarse and baked by the sun.

The little white-striped nigger nibbles at the lettuce-leaf I give him, and leaps about gaily in the cage where I have housed him. I could easily rear him, but he would not teach me much more. So I restore him to liberty. In return for what he has taught me I give him the grass and the Locusts in the garden.

For he taught me that Grasshoppers, in order to leave the ground where the eggs are laid, wear a temporary form which keeps those too cumbrous parts, the long legs and antennæ, swathed together in a sheath. He taught me, too, that this mummy-like creature, fit only to lengthen and shorten itself a little, has for its means of travelling a hernia in the neck, a throb-bing blister—an original piece of mechanism which, when I first observed the Decticus, I had never seen used as an aid to pro-gression.

CHAPTER X

Common Wasps

I

Their Cleverness and Stupidity

Wishing to observe a Wasp's nest I go out, one day in September, with my little son Paul, who helps me with his good sight and his undivided attention. We look with interest at the edges of the footpaths.

Suddenly Paul cries: "A Wasp's nest! A Wasp's nest, as sure as anything!" For, twenty yards away, he has seen rising from the ground, shooting up and flying away, now one and then another swiftly moving object, as though some tiny crater in the grass were hurling them forth.

We approach the spot with caution, fearing to attract the attention of the fierce creatures. At the entrance-door of their dwelling, a round opening large enough to admit a man's thumb, the inmates come and go, busily passing one another as they fly in opposite directions. *Burr!* A shudder runs through me at the thought of the unpleasant time we should have, did we incite these irritable warriors to attack us by inspecting them too closely. Without further investigation, which might cost us too dear, we mark the spot, and resolve to return at nightfall. By that time all the inhabitants of the nest will have come home from the fields.

The conquest of a nest of Common Wasps would be rather a serious undertaking if one did not act with a certain amount of prudence. Half a pint of petrol, a reed-stump nine inches long, and a good-sized lump of clay or loam, kneaded to the right consistency—such are my weapons, which I have come to consider the best and simplest, after various trials with less successful means.

The suffocating method is necessary, unless I use costly measures which I cannot afford. When Réaumur wanted to place a live Wasp's nest in a glass case with a view to observing the habits of the inmates, he employed helpers who were used to the painful job, and were willing, for a handsome reward, to serve the man of science at the cost of their skins. But I, who should have to pay with my own skin, think twice before digging up the nest I desire. I begin by suffocating the inhabitants. Dead Wasps do not sting. It is a brutal method, but perfectly safe.

I use petrol because its effects are not too violent, and in order to make my observations I wish to leave a small number of survivors. The question is how to introduce it into the cavity containing the Wasp's nest. A vestibule, or entrance-passage, about nine inches long, and very nearly horizontal, leads to the underground cells. To pour the petrol straight into the mouths of this tunnel would be a blunder that might have serious consequences later on. For so small a quantity of petrol would be absorbed by the soil and would never reach the nest; and next day, when we might think we were digging safely, we should find an infuriated swarm under the spade.

The bit of reed prevents this mishap. When inserted into the passage it forms a water-tight funnel, and carries the petrol to the cavern without the loss of a drop, and as quickly as possible. Then we fix the lump of kneaded clay into the entrance-hole, like a stopper. We have nothing to do now but wait.

When we are going to perform this operation Paul and I set out, carrying a lantern and a basket with the implements, at nine o'clock on some mild, moonlit evening. While the farm-house Dogs are yelping at each other in the distance, and the Screech Owl is hooting in the olive-trees, and the Italian Crickets are performing their symphony in the bushes, Paul and I chat about insects. He asks questions, eager to learn, and I tell him the little that I know. So delightful are our nights of Wasp-hunting that we think little of the loss of sleep or the chance of being stung!

The pushing of the reed into the hole is the most delicate matter. Since the direction of the passage is unknown there is some hesitation, and sometimes sentries come flying out of the

Wasp's guard-house to attack the operator's hand. To prevent this one of us keeps watch, and drives away the enemy with a handkerchief. And after all, a swelling on one's hand, even if it does smart, is not much to pay for an idea.

As the petrol streams into the cavern we hear the threatening buzz of the population underground. Then quick!—the door must be closed with the wet clay, and the clod kicked once or twice with the heel to make the stopper solid. There is nothing more to be done for the present. Off we go to bed.

With a spade and a trowel we are back on the spot at dawn. It is wise to be early, because many Wasps will have been out all night, and will want to get into their home while we are digging. The chill of the morning will make them less fierce.

In front of the entrance-passage, in which the reed is still sticking, we dig a trench wide enough to allow us free movement. Then the side of this ditch is carefully cut away, slice after slice, until, at a depth of about twenty inches, the Wasp's nest is revealed, uninjured, slung from the roof of a spacious cavity.

It is indeed a superb achievement, as large as a fair-sized pumpkin. It hangs free on every side except at the top, where various roots, mostly of couch-grass, penetrate the thickness of the wall and fasten the nest firmly. Its shape is round wherever the ground has been soft, and of the same consistency all through. In stony soil, where the Wasps meet with obstacles in their digging, the sphere becomes more or less misshapen.

A space of a hand's-breadth is always left open between the paper nest and the sides of the underground vault. This space is the wide street along which the builders move unhindered at their continual task of enlarging and strengthening the nest, and the passage that leads to the outer world opens into it. Underneath the nest is a much larger unoccupied space, rounded into a big basin, so that the wrapper of the nest can be enlarged as fresh cells are added. This cavity also serves as a dust-bin for refuse.

The cavity was dug by the Wasps themselves. Of that there is no doubt; for holes so large and so regular do not exist ready-made. The original foundress of the nest may have seized on some cavity made by a Mole, to help her at the beginning; but the greater part of the enormous vault was the work of the Wasps. Yet there is not a scrap of rubbish outside the entrance. Where is the mass of earth that has been removed?

It has been spread over such a large surface of ground that it is unnoticed. Thousands and thousands of Wasps work at digging the cellar, and enlarging it as that becomes necessary. They fly up to the outer world, each carrying a particle of earth, which they drop on the ground at some distance from the nest, in all directions. Being scattered in this way the earth leaves no visible trace.

The Wasp's nest is made of a thin, flexible material like brown paper, formed of particles of wood. It is streaked with bands, of which the colour varies according to the wood used. If it were made in a single continuous sheet it would give little protection against the cold. But the Common Wasp, like the balloon-maker, knows that heat may be preserved by means of a cushion of air contained by several wrappers. So she makes her paper-pulp into broad scales, which overlap loosely and are laid on in numerous layers. The whole forms a coarse blanket, thick and spongy in texture and well filled with stagnant air. The temperature under this shelter must be truly tropical in hot weather.

The fierce Hornet, chief of the Wasps, builds her nest on the same principle. In the hollow of a willow, or within some empty granary, she makes, out of fragments of wood, a very brittle kind of striped yellow cardboard. Her nest is wrapped round with many layers of this substance, laid on in the form of broad convex scales which are welded to one another. Between them are wide intervals in which air is held motionless.

The Wasp, then, often acts in accordance with the laws of physics and geometry. She employs air, a non-conductor of heat, to keep her home warm; she made blankets before man thought of it; she builds the outer walls of the nest in the shape that gives her the largest amount of room in the smallest wrapper; and in the form of her cell, too, she economises space and material.

And yet, clever as these wonderful architects are, they amaze us by their stupidity in the face of the smallest difficulty. On the one hand their instincts teach them to behave like men of science; but on the other it is plain that they are entirely without the power of reflection. I have convinced myself of this fact by various experiments.

The Common Wasp has chanced to set up house beside one of the walks in my enclosure, which enables me to experiment with a bell-glass. In the open fields I could not use this appliance, because the boys of the country-side would soon smash it. One night, when all was dark and the Wasps had gone home, I placed the glass over the entrance of the burrow, after first flattening the soil. When the Wasps began work again next morning and found themselves checked in their flight, would they succeed in making a passage under the rim of the glass? Would these sturdy creatures, who were capable of digging a spacious cavern, realise that a very short underground tunnel would set them free? That was the question.

The next morning I found the bright sunlight falling on the bell-glass, and the workers ascending in crowds from underground, eager to go in search of provisions. They butted against the transparent wall, tumbled down, picked themselves up again, and whirled round and round in a crazy swarm. Some, weary of dancing, wandered peevishly at random and then re-entered their dwelling. Others took their places as the sun grew hotter. But not one of them, not a single one, scratched with her feet at the base of the glass circle. This means of escape was beyond them.

Meanwhile a few Wasps who had spent the night out of doors were coming in from the fields. Round and round the bell-glass they flew; and at last, after much hesitation, one of them decided to dig under the edge. Others followed her example, a passage was easily opened, and the Wasps went in. Then I closed the passage with some earth. The narrow opening, if seen from within, might help the Wasps to escape, and I wished to leave the prisoners the honour of winning their liberty.

However poor the Wasps' power of reasoning, I thought their escape was now probable. Those who had just entered would surely show the way; they would teach the others to dig below the wall of glass.

I was too hasty. Of learning by experience or example there was not a sign. Inside the glass not an attempt was made to dig a tunnel. The insect population whirled round and round, but showed no enterprise. They floundered about, while every day numbers died from famine and heat. At the end of a week not one was left alive. A heap of corpses covered the ground.

The Wasps returning from the field could find their way in, because the power of scenting their house through the soil, and searching for it, is one of their natural instincts, one of the means of defence given to them. There is no need for thought or reasoning here: the earthy obstacle has been familiar to every Wasp since Wasps first came into the world.

But those who are within the bell-glass have no such instinct to help them. Their aim is to get into the light, and finding daylight in their transparent prison they think their aim is accomplished. In spite of constant collisions with the glass they spend themselves in vainly trying to fly farther in the direction of the sunshine. There is nothing in the past to teach them what to do. They keep blindly to their familiar habits, and die.

II

Some of Their Habits

If we open the thick envelope of the nest we shall find, inside, a number of combs, or layers of cells, lying one below the other and fastened together by solid pillars. The number of these layers varies. Towards the end of the season there may be ten, or even more. The opening of the cells is on the lower surface. In this strange world the young grow, sleep, and receive their food head downwards.

The various storeys, or layers of combs, are divided by open spaces; and between the outer envelope and the stack of combs there are doorways through which every part can be easily reached. There is a continual coming and going of nurses, attending to the grubs in the cells. On one side of the outer wrapper is the gate of the city, a modest unadorned opening, lost among the thin scales of the envelope. Facing it is the entrance to the tunnel that leads from the cavity to the world at large.

In a Wasp community there is a large number of Wasps whose

whole life is spent in work. It is their business to enlarge the nest as the population grows; and though they have no grubs of their own, they nurse the grubs in the cells with the greatest care and industry. Wishing to watch their operations, and also to see what would take place at the approach of winter, I placed under cover one October a few fragments of a nest, containing a large number of eggs and grubs, with about a hundred workers to take care of them.

To make my inspection easier I separated the combs and placed them side by side, with the openings of the cells turned upwards. This arrangement, the reverse of the usual position, did not seem to annoy my prisoners, who soon recovered from the disturbance and set to work as if nothing had happened. In case they should wish to build I gave them a slip of soft wood; and I fed them with honey. The underground cave in which the nest hangs out of doors was represented by a large earthen pan under a wire-gauze cover. A removable cardboard dome provided darkness for the Wasps, and—when removed—light for me.

The Wasps' work went on as if it had never been interrupted. The worker-Wasps attended to the grubs and the building at the same time. They began to raise a wall round the most thickly populated combs; and it seemed as though they might intend to build a new envelope, to replace the one ruined by my spade. But they were not repairing; they were simply carrying on the work from the point at which I interrupted it. Over about a third of the comb they made an arched roof of paper scales, which would have been joined to the envelope of the nest if it had been intact. The tent they made sheltered only a small part of the disk of cells.

As for the wood I provided for them, they did not touch it. To this raw material, which would have been troublesome to work, they preferred the old cells that were no longer in use. In these the fibres were already prepared; and, with a little saliva and a little grinding in their mandibles, they turned them into pulp of the highest quality. The uninhabited cells were nibbled into pieces, and out of the ruins a sort of canopy was built. New cells could be made in the same way if necessary.

Even more interesting than this roofing-work is the feeding of

the grubs. One could never weary of the sight of the rough fight-
ers turned into tender nurses. The barracks become a *crêche*.
With what care those grubs are reared! If we watch one of the
busy Wasps we shall see her, with her crop swollen with honey,
halt in front of a cell. With a thoughtful air she bends her head
into the opening, and touches the grub with the tip of her anten-
na. The grub wakes and gapes at her, like a fledgling when the
mother-bird returns to the nest with food.

For a moment the awakened larva swings its head to and fro:
it is blind, and is trying to feel the food brought to it. The two
mouths meet; a drop of syrup passes from the nurse's mouth to
the nurseling's. That is enough for the moment: now for the next
Wasp-baby. The nurse moves on, to continue her duties elsewhere.

Meanwhile the grub is licking the base of its own neck. For,
while it is being fed, there appears a temporary swelling on its
chest, which acts as a bib, and catches whatever trickles down
from the mouth. After swallowing the chief part of the meal the
grub gathers up the crumbs that have fallen on its bib. Then the
swelling disappears; and the grub, withdrawing a little way into
its cell, resumes its sweet slumbers.

When fed in my cage the Wasp-grubs have their heads up,
and what falls from their mouths collects naturally on their bibs.
When fed in the nest they have their heads down. But I have no
doubt that even in this position the bib serves its purpose.

By slightly bending its head the grub can always deposit on
the projecting bib a portion of the overflowing mouthful, which
is sticky enough to remain there. Moreover, it is quite possible
that the nurse herself places a portion of her helping on this
spot. Whether it be above or below the mouth, right way up or
upside down, the bib fulfils its office because of the sticky
nature of the food. It is a temporary saucer which shortens the
work of serving out the rations, and enables the grub to feed in
a more or less leisurely fashion and without too much gluttony.

In the open country, late in the year when fruit is scarce, the
grubs are mostly fed upon minced Fly; but in my cages everything is refused but honey. Both nurses and nurselings seem to
thrive on this diet, and if any intruder ventures too near to the

combs he is doomed. Wasps, it appears, are far from hospitable. Even the Polistes, an insect who is absolutely like a Wasp in shape and colour, is at once recognised and mobbed if she approaches the honey the Wasps are sipping. Her appearance takes nobody in for a moment, and unless she hastily retires she will meet with a violent death. No, it is not a good thing to enter a Wasps' nest, even when the stranger wears the same uniform, pursues the same industry, and is almost a member of the same corporation.

Again and again I have seen the savage reception given to strangers. If the stranger be of sufficient importance he is stabbed, and his body is dragged from the nest and flung into the refuse-heap below. But the poisoned dagger seems to be reserved for great occasions. If I throw the grub of a Saw-fly among the Wasps they show great surprise at the black-and-green dragon; they snap at it boldly, and wound it, but without stinging it. They try to haul it away. The dragon resists, anchoring itself to the comb by its hooks, holding on now by its fore-legs and now by its hind-legs. At last the grub, however, weakened by its wounds, is torn from the comb and dragged bleeding to the refuse-pit. It has taken a couple of hours to dislodge it.

Supposing, on the other hand, I throw on to the combs a certain imposing grub that lives under the bark of cherry-trees, five or six Wasps will at once prick it with their stings. In a couple of minutes it is dead. But the huge dead body is much too heavy to be carried out of the nest. So the Wasps, finding they cannot move the grub, eat it where it lies, or at least reduce its weight till they can drag the remains outside the walls.

III

Their Sad End

Protected in this fierce way against the invasion of intruders, and fed with excellent honey, the grubs in my cage prosper greatly. But of course there are exceptions. In the Wasps' nest, as everywhere, there are weaklings who are cut down before their time.

I see these puny sufferers refuse their food and slowly pine away. The nurses perceive it even more clearly. They bend their heads over the invalid, sound it with their antennæ, and pronounce it incurable. Then the creature at the point of death is torn ruthlessly from its cell and dragged outside the nest. In the brutal commonwealth of the Wasps the invalid is merely a piece of rubbish, to be got rid of as soon as possible for fear of contagion. Nor indeed is this the worst. As winter draws near the Wasps foresee their fate. They know their end is at hand.

The first cold nights of November bring a change in the nest. The building proceeds with diminished enthusiasm; the visits to the pool of honey are less constant. Household duties are relaxed. Grubs gaping with hunger receive tardy relief, or are even neglected. Profound uneasiness seizes upon the nurses. Their former devotion is succeeded by indifference, which soon turns to dislike. What is the good of continuing attentions which soon will be impossible? A time of famine is coming; the nurselings in any case must die a tragic death. So the tender nurses become savage executioners.

"Let us leave no orphans," they say to themselves; "no one would care for them after we are gone. Let us kill everything, eggs and grubs alike. A violent end is better than a slow death by starvation."

A massacre follows. The grubs are seized by the scruff of the neck, brutally torn from their cells, dragged out of the nest, and thrown into the refuse-heap at the bottom of the cave. The nurses, or workers, root them out of their cells as violently as though they were strangers or dead bodies. They tug at them savagely and tear them. Then the eggs are ripped open and devoured.

Before much longer the nurses themselves, the executioners, are languidly dragging what remains of their lives. Day by day, with a curiosity mingled with emotion, I watch the end of my insects. The workers die suddenly. They come to the surface, slip down, fall on their backs and rise no more, as if they were struck by lightning. They have had their day; they are slain by age, that merciless poison. Even so does a piece of clockwork become motionless when its mainspring has unwound its last spiral.

The workers are old: but the mothers are the last to be born into the nest, and have all the vigour of youth. And so, when winter sickness seizes them, they are capable of a certain resistance. Those whose end is near are easily distinguished from the others by the disorder of their appearance. Their backs are dusty. While they are well they dust themselves without ceasing, and their black-and-yellow coats are kept perfectly glossy. Those who are ailing are careless of cleanliness; they stand motionless in the sun or wander languidly about. They no longer brush their clothes.

This indifference to dress is a bad sign. Two or three days later the dusty female leaves the nest for the last time. She goes outside, to enjoy yet a little of the sunlight; presently she slides quietly to the ground and does not get up again. She declines to die in her beloved paper home, where the code of the Wasps ordains absolute cleanliness. The dying Wasp performs her own funeral rites by dropping herself into the pit at the bottom of the cavern. For reasons of health these stoics refuse to die in the actual house, among the combs. The last survivors retain this repugnance to the very end. It is a law that never falls into disuse, however greatly reduced the population may be.

My cage becomes emptier day by day, notwithstanding the mildness of the room, and notwithstanding the saucer of honey at which the able-bodied come to sip. At Christmas I have only a dozen females left. On the sixth of January the last of them perishes.

Whence arises this mortality, which mows down the whole of my wasps? They have not suffered from famine: they have not suffered from cold: they have not suffered from home-sickness. Then what have they died of?

We must not blame their captivity. The same thing happens in the open country. Various nests I have inspected at the end of December all show the same condition. The vast majority of Wasps must die, apparently, not by accident, nor illness, nor the inclemency of the season, but by an inevitable destiny, which destroys them as energetically as it brings them into life. And it is well for us that it is so. One female Wasp is enough to found a city of thirty thousand inhabitants. If all were to survive, what a scourge they would be! The Wasps would tyrannise over the countryside.

In the end the nest itself perishes. A certain Caterpillar which later on becomes a mean-looking Moth; a tiny reddish Beetle; and a scaly grub clad in gold velvet, are the creatures that demolish it. They gnaw the floors of the various storeys, and crumble the whole dwelling. A few pinches of dust, a few shreds of brown paper are all that remain, by the return of spring, of the Wasps' city and its thirty thousand inhabitants.

CHAPTER XI

The Adventures of a Grub

I

The Young Sitaris

The high banks of sandy clay in the country round about Carpentras are the favourite haunts of a host of Bees and Wasps, those lovers of a sunny aspect and of soil that is easy to dig in. Here, in the month of May, two Bees, both of them Mason-bees, builders of subterranean cells, are especially abundant. One of them builds at the entrance of her dwelling an advanced fortification, an earthly cylinder, wrought in open work and curved, of the width and length of a man's finger. When it is peopled with many Bees one stands amazed at the elaborate ornamentation formed by all these hanging fingers of clay.

The other Bee, who is very much more frequently seen and is called *Anthophora pilipes,* leaves the opening of her corridor bare. The chinks between the stones in old walls and abandoned hovels, or exposed surfaces of sand stone or marl, are found suitable for her labours; but the favourite spots, those to which the greatest number of swarms resort, are straight stretches of ground exposed to the south, such as occur in the cuttings of deeply-sunken roads. Here, over areas many yards in width, the wall is drilled with a multitude of holes, which give to the earthy mass the look of some enormous sponge. These round holes might have been made with a gimlet, so regular are they. Each is the entrance to a winding corridor, which runs to the depth of four or five inches. The cells are at the far end. If we wish to watch the labours of the industrious Bee we must visit her workshop during the latter half of May. Then—but at a respectful distance—we may see, in all its bewildering activity, the tumul-

tuous, buzzing swarm, busied with the building and provisioning of the cells.

But it has been most often during the months of August and
September, the happy months of the summer holidays, that I
have visited the banks inhabited by the Anthophora. At this season all is silent near the nests: the work has long been completed: and numbers of Spiders' webs line the crevices or plunge
their silken tubes into the Bees' corridors. That is no reason,
however, for hastily abandoning the city that was once so full of
life and bustle, and now appears deserted. A few inches below
the surface, thousands of grubs are imprisoned in their cells of
clay, resting until the coming spring. Surely these grubs, which
are paralysed and incapable of self-defence, must be a temptation—fat little morsels as they are—to some kind of parasite,
some kind of insect stranger in search of prey. The matter is
worth inquiring into.

Two facts are at once noticeable. Some dismal-looking Flies,
half black and half white, are flying indolently from gallery to
gallery, evidently with the object of laying their eggs there.
Many of them are hanging dry and lifeless in the Spiders' webs.
At other places the entire surface of a bank is hung with the
dried corpses of a certain Beetle, called the Sitaris. Among the
corpses, however, are a few live Beetles, both male and female.
The female Beetle invariably disappears into the Bees' dwelling.
Without a doubt she, too, lays her eggs there.

If we give a few blows of the pick to the surface of the bank
we shall find out something more about these things. During
the early days of August this is what we shall see: the cells forming the top layer are unlike those at a greater depth. The difference is owing to the fact that the same establishment is used by
two kinds of Bee, the Anthophora and the Osmia.

The Anthophoræ are the actual pioneers. The work of boring
the galleries is wholly theirs, and their cells are right at the end.
If they, for any reason, leave the outer cells, the Osmia comes in
and takes possession of them. She divides the corridors into
unequal and inartistic cells by means of rough earthen partitions, her only idea of masonry.

The cells of the Anthophora are faultlessly regular and per-

fectly finished. They are works of art, cut out of the very substance of the earth, well out of reach of all ordinary enemies;
and for this reason the larva of this Bee has no means of spinning a cocoon. It lies naked in the cell, whose inner surface is
polished like stucco.

In the Osmia's cells, however, means of defence are required,
because they are at the surface of the soil, are roughly made,
and are badly protected by their thin partitions. So the Osmia's
grubs enclose themselves in a very strong cocoon, which preserves them both from the rough sides of their shapeless cells
and from the jaws of various enemies who prowl about the galleries. It is easy, then, in a bank inhabited by these two Bees, to
recognise the cells belonging to each. The Anthophora's cells
contain a naked grub: those of the Osmia contain a grub
enclosed in a cocoon.

Now each of these two Bees has its own especial parasite, or
uninvited guest. The parasite of the Osmia is the black-and-
white Fly who is to be seen so often at the entrance to the galleries, intent on laying her eggs within them. The parasite of the
Anthophora is the Sitaris, the Beetle whose corpses appear in
such quantities on the surface of the bank.

If the layer of Osmia-cells be removed from the nest we can
observe the cells of the Anthophora. Some will be occupied by
larvæ, some by the perfect insect, and some—indeed many—
will contain a singular egg-shaped shell, divided into segments
with projecting breathing-pores. This shell is extremely thin and
fragile; it is amber-coloured, and so transparent that one can distinguish quite plainly through its sides a full-grown Sitaris,
struggling as though to set herself at liberty.

What is this curious shell, which does not appear to be a
Beetle's shell at all? And how can this parasite reach a cell which
seems to be inaccessible because of its position, and in which
the most careful examination under the magnifying-glass reveals
no sign of violence? Three years of close observation enabled
me to answer these questions, and to add one of its most astonishing chapters to the story of insect life. Here is the result of my
inquiries.

The Sitaris in the full-grown state lives only for a day or two, and its whole life is passed at the entrance to the Anthophora's galleries. It has no concern but the reproduction of the species. It is provided with the usual digestive organs, but I have grave reasons to doubt whether it actually takes any nourishment whatever. The female's only thought is to lay her eggs. This done, she dies. The male, after cowering in a crevice for a day or two, also perishes. This is the origin of all those corpses swinging in the Spiders' web, with which the neighbourhood of the Anthophora's dwelling is upholstered.

At first sight one would expect that the Sitaris, when laying her eggs, would go from cell to cell, confiding an egg to each of the Bee-grubs. But when, in the course of my observations, I searched the Bees' galleries, I invariably found the eggs of the Sitaris gathered in a heap inside the entrance, at a distance of an inch or two from the opening. They are white, oval, and very small, and they stick together slightly. As for their number, I do not believe I am exaggerating when I estimate it at two thousand at least.

Thus, contrary to what one was to some extent entitled to suppose, the eggs are not laid in the cells of the Bee; they are simply dumped in a heap inside the doorway of her dwelling. Nay more, the mother does not make any protective structure for them; she takes no pains to shield them from the rigours of winter; she does not even attempt to stop up the entrance-lobby in which she has placed them, and so protect them from the thousand enemies that threaten them. For as long as the frosts of winter have not arrived these open galleries are trodden by Spiders and other plunderers, for whom the eggs would make an agreeable meal.

The better to observe them, I placed a number of the eggs in boxes; and when they hatched out about the end of September I imagined they would at once start off in search of an Anthophora-cell. I was entirely wrong. The young grubs—little black creatures no more than the twenty-fifth of an inch long—did not move away, though provided with vigorous legs. They remained higgledy-piggledy, mixed up with the skins of the eggs whence they came. In vain I placed within their reach lumps of earth containing open Bee-cells: nothing would tempt them to move. If I forcibly removed a few from the common heap they at once hurried back to it in order to hide themselves among the rest.

At last, to assure myself that the Sitaris-grubs, in the free state, do not disperse after they are hatched, I went in the winter to Carpentras and inspected the banks inhabited by the Anthophoræ. There, as in my boxes, I found the grubs all piled up in heaps, all mixed up with the skins of the eggs.

I was no nearer answering the question: how does the Sitaris get into the Bees' cells, and into a shell that does not belong to it?

II

The First Adventure

The appearance of the young Sitaris showed me at once that its habits must be peculiar. It could not, I saw, be called on to move on an ordinary surface. The spot where this larva has to live evidently exposes it to the risk of many dangerous falls, since, in order to prevent them, it is equipped with a pair of powerful mandibles, curved and sharp; robust legs which end in a long and very mobile claw; a variety of bristles and probes; and a couple of strong spikes with sharp, hard points—an elaborate mechanism, like a sort of plough-share, capable of biting into the most highly polished surface. Nor is this all. It is further provided with a sticky liquid, sufficiently adhesive to hold it in position without the help of other appliances. In vain I racked my brains to guess what the substance might be, so shifting, so uncertain, and so perilous, which the young Sitaris is destined to inhabit. I waited with eager impatience for the return of the warm weather.

At the end of April the young grubs imprisoned in my cages, hitherto lying motionless and hidden in the spongy heap of egg-skins, suddenly began to move. They scattered, and ran about in all directions through the boxes and jars in which they have passed the winter. Their hurried movements and untiring energy showed they were in search of something, and the natural thing for them to seek was food. For these grubs were hatched at the end of September, and since then, that is to say for seven long months, they had taken no nourishment, although they were by no means in a state of torpor. From the moment of their hatching they are doomed, though full of life, to an absolute fast lasting for seven months; and when I saw their excitement I naturally supposed that an imperious hunger had set them bustling in that fashion.

The food they desired could only be the contents of the Anthophora's cells, since at a later stage the Sitaris is found in those cells. Now these contents are limited to honey and Bee-grubs.

I offered them some cells containing larvæ: I even slipped the Sitares into the cells, and did all sorts of things to tempt their appetite. My efforts were fruitless. Then I tried honey. In hunting for cells provisioned with honey I lost a good part of the month of May. Having found them I removed the Bee-grub from some of them, and laid the Sitaris-grub on the surface of the honey. Never did experiment break down so completely! Far from eating the honey, the grubs became entangled in the sticky mass and perished in it, suffocated. "I have offered you larvæ, cells, honey!" I cried in despair. "Then what do you want, you fiendish little creatures?"

Well, in the end I found out what they wanted. They wanted the Anthophora herself to carry them into the cells!

When April comes, as I said before, the heap of grubs at the entrance to the Bees' cells begins to show signs of activity. A few days later they are no longer there. Strange as it may appear, they are all careering about the country, sometimes at a great distance, clinging like grim death to the fleece of a Bee!

When the Anthophoræ pass by the entrance to their cells, on their way either in or out, the young Sitaris-grub, who is lying in wait there, attaches himself to one of the Bees. He wriggles into the fur and clutches it so firmly that he need not fear a fall during the long journeys of the insect that carries him. By thus attaching himself to the Bee the Sitaris intends to get himself carried, at the right moment, into a cell supplied with honey.

One might at first sight believe that these adventurous grubs derive food for a time from the Bee's body. But not at all. The young Sitares, embedded in the fleece, at right angles to the body of the Anthophora, head inwards, tail outwards, do not stir from the spot they have selected, a point near the Bee's shoulders. We do not see them wandering from spot to spot, exploring the Bee's body, seeking the part where the skin is most delicate, as they would certainly do if they were really feeding on the insect. On the contrary, they are always fixed on the toughest and hardest part of the Bee's body, a little below the insertion of the wings, or sometimes on the head; and they remain absolutely motionless, clinging to a single hair. It seems to me undeniable that the young Sitares settle on the Bee merely to make her carry them into the cells that she will soon be building.

But in the meantime the future parasites must hold tight to the fleece of their hostess, in spite of her rapid flights among the flowers, in spite of her rubbing against the walls of the galleries when she enters to take shelter, and in spite, above all, of the brushing which she must often give herself with her feet, to dust herself and keep spick and span. We were wondering a little time ago what the dangerous, shifting thing could be on which the grub would have to establish itself. That thing is the hair of a Bee who makes a thousand rapid journeys, now diving into her narrow galleries, now forcing her way down the tight throat of a flower.

We can now quite understand the use of the two spikes, which close together and are able to take hold of hair more easily than the most delicate tweezers. We can see the full value of the sticky liquid that helps the tiny creature to hold fast; and we can realise that the elastic probes and bristles on the legs serve to penetrate the Bee's down and anchor the grub in position. The more one considers this arrangement, which seems so useless as the grub drags itself laboriously over a smooth surface, the more does one marvel at all the machinery which this fragile creature carries about to save it from falling during its adventurous rides.

III

The Second Adventure

One 21st of May I went to Carpentras, determined to see, if possible, the entrance of the Sitaris into the Bee's cells.

The works were in full swing. In front of a high expanse of earth a swarm of Bees, stimulated by the sun, was dancing a crazy ballet. From the tumultuous heart of the cloud rose a monotonous, threatening murmur, while my bewildered eye tried to follow the movements of the throng. Quick as a lightning-flash thousands of Anthophoræ were flying hither and thither in search of booty: thousands of others, also, were arriving, laden with honey, or with mortar for their building.

At that time I knew comparatively little about these insects. It seemed to me that any one who ventured into the swarm, or—above all—who laid a rash hand on the Bees' dwellings, would instantly be stabbed by a thousand stings. I had once observed the combs of the Hornet too closely; and a shiver of fear passed through me.

Yet, to find out what I wished to know, I must needs penetrate that fearsome swarm; I must stand for whole hours, perhaps all day, watching the works I intended to upset; lens in hand, I must examine, unmoved amid the whirl, the things that were happening in the cells. Moreover, the use of a mask, of gloves, of a covering of any kind, was out of the question, for my fingers and eyes must be absolutely free. No matter: even though I should leave the Bee's nest with my face swollen beyond recognition, I was determined that day to solve the problem that had puzzled me too long.

Having caught a few stray Anthophoræ with my net, I satisfied myself that the Sitaris-larvæ were perched, as I expected, on the Bees.

I buttoned my coat tightly and entered the heart of the swarm. With a few blows of the mattock I secured a lump of earth, and to my great surprise found myself uninjured. A second expedition, longer than the first, had the same result: not a Bee touched me with her sting. After this I remained permanently in front of the nest, removing lumps of earth, spilling the honey, and crushing the Bees, without arousing anything worse than a louder hum. For the Anthophora is a pacific creature. When disturbed in the cells it leaves them hastily and escapes, sometimes even mortally wounded, without using its venomous sting except when it is seized and handled.

Thanks to this unexpected lack of spirit in the Mason-bee, I was able for hours to investigate her cells at my leisure, seated on a stone in the midst of the murmuring and distracted swarm, without receiving a single sting, though I took no precautions whatever. Country folk, happening to pass and seeing me seated thus calmly amid the Bees, stopped aghast to ask me if I had bewitched them.

In this way I examined the cells. Some were still open, and contained only a more or less complete store of honey. Others were closely sealed with an earthen lid. The contents of these varied greatly. Sometimes I found the larva of a Bee; sometimes another, fatter kind of larva; at other times honey with an egg floating on the surface. The egg was of a beautiful white, and was shaped like a cylinder with a slight curve, a fifth or sixth of an inch in length—the egg of the Anthophora.

In a few cells I found this egg floating all alone on the surface of the honey: in others, very many others, I saw, lying on the Bee's egg as though on a sort of raft, a young Sitaris-grub. Its shape and size were those of the creature when it is hatched. Here, then, was the enemy within the gates.

When and how did it get in? In none of the cells was I able to detect any chink by which it could have entered: they were all sealed quite tightly. The parasite must have established itself in the honey-warehouse before the warehouse was closed. On the other hand, the open cells, full of honey but as yet without an egg, never contain a Sitaris. The grub must therefore gain admittance either while the Bee is laying the egg, or else afterwards, while she is busy plastering up the door. My experiments have convinced me that the Sitaris enters the cell in the very second when the egg is laid on the surface of the honey.

If I take a cell full of honey, with an egg floating in it, and place it in a glass tube with some Sitaris-grubs, they very rarely venture inside it. They cannot reach the raft in safety: the honey that surrounds it is too dangerous. If one of them by chance approaches the honey it tries to escape as soon as it sees the sticky nature of the stuff under its feet. It often ends by falling back into the cell, where it dies of suffocation. It is therefore certain that the grub does not leave the fleece of the Bee when the latter is in her cell or near it, in order to make a rush for the honey; for this honey would inevitably cause its death, if it so much as touched the surface.

We must remember that the young Sitaris which is found in a closed cell is always placed on the egg of the Bee. This egg not only serves as a raft for the tiny creature floating on a very treacherous lake, but also provides it with its first meal. To get at this egg, in the centre of the lake of honey, to reach this raft which is also its first food, the young grub must somehow contrive to avoid the fatal touch of the honey.

There is only one way in which this can be done. The clever grub, at the very moment when the Bee is laying her egg, slips off the Bee and on to the egg, and with it reaches the surface of the honey. The egg is too small to hold more than one grub, and that is why we never find more than one Sitaris in a cell. Such a performance on the part of a grub seems extraordinarily inspired—but then the study of insects constantly gives us examples of such inspiration.

When dropping her egg upon the honey, then, the Anthophora at the same time drops into her cell the mortal enemy of her race. She carefully plasters the lid which closes the entrance to the cell, and all is done. A second cell is built beside it, probably to suffer the same fate; and so on until all the parasites sheltered by her fleece are comfortably housed. Let us leave the unhappy mother to continue her fruitless task, and turn our attention to the young larva which has so cleverly secured for itself board and lodging.

Let us suppose that we remove the lid from a cell in which the egg, recently laid, supports a Sitaris-grub. The egg is intact and in perfect condition. But now the work of destruction begins. The grub, a tiny black speck which we see running over the white surface of the egg, at last stops and balances itself firmly on its six legs; then, seizing the delicate skin of the egg with the sharp hooks of its mandibles, it tugs at it violently till it breaks and spills the contents. These contents the grub eagerly drinks up. Thus the first stroke of the parasite's mandibles is aimed at the destruction of the Bee's egg.

This is a very wise precaution on the part of the Sitaris-grub! It will have to feed on the honey in the cell: the Bee's grub which would come out of the egg would also require the honey: there is not enough for two. So—quick!—a bite at the egg, and the difficulty is removed.

Moreover, another reason for the destruction of the egg is that special tastes compel the young Sitaris to make its first meals of it. The tiny creature begins by greedily drinking the juices which the torn wrapper of the egg allows to escape. For several days it continues to rip the envelope gradually open, and to feed on the liquid that trickles from it. Meanwhile it never touches the honey that surrounds it. The Bee's egg is absolutely necessary to the Sitaris-grub, not merely as a boat, but also as nourishment.

At the end of a week the egg is nothing but a dry skin. The first meal is finished. The Sitaris-grub, which is now twice as large as before, splits open along the back, and through this slit the second form of this singular Beetle falls on the surface of the honey. Its cast skin remains on the raft, and will presently disappear with it beneath the waves of honey.

Here ends the history of the first form adopted by the Sitaris.

CHAPTER XII

The Cricket

I

The Householder

The Field Cricket, the inhabitant of the meadows, is almost as famous as the Cicada, and figures among the limited but glorious number of the classic insects. He owes this honour to his song and his house. One thing alone is lacking to complete his renown. The master of the art of making animals talk, La Fontaine, gives him hardly two lines.

Florian, the other French writer of fables, gives us a story of a Cricket, but it lacks the simplicity of truth and the saving salt of humour. Besides, it represents the Cricket as discontented, bewailing his condition! This is a preposterous idea, for all who have studied him know, on the contrary, that he is very well pleased with his own talent and his own burrow. And indeed, at the end of the story, Florian makes him admit:

> "My snug little home is a place of delight;
> If you want to live happy, live hidden from sight!"

I find more force and truth in some verses by a friend of mine, of which these are a translation:

> Among the beasts a tale is told
>   How a poor Cricket ventured nigh
> His door to catch the sun's warm gold
>   And saw a radiant Butterfly.
>
> She passed with tails thrown proudly back
>   And long gay rows of crescents blue,

Brave yellow stars and bands of black,
    The lordliest Fly that ever flew.

"Ah, fly away," the hermit said,
    "Daylong among your flowers to roam;
Nor daisies white nor roses red
    Will compensate my lowly home."

True, all too true! There came a storm
    And caught the Fly within its flood,
Staining her broken velvet form
    And covering her wings with mud.

The Cricket, sheltered from the rain,
    Chirped, and looked on with tranquil eye;
For him the thunder pealed in vain,
    The gale and torrent passed him by.

Then shun the world, nor take your fill
    Of any of its joys or flowers;
A lowly fire-side, calm and still,
    At least will grant you tearless hours![1]

There I recognise my Cricket. I see him curling his antennæ on the threshold of his burrow, keeping himself cool in front and warm at the back. He is not jealous of the Butterfly; on the contrary, he pities her, with that air of mocking commiseration we often see in those who have houses of their own when they are talking to those who have none. Far from complaining, he is very well satisfied both with his house and his violin. He is a true philosopher: he knows the vanity of things and feels the charm of a modest retreat away from the riot of pleasure-seekers.

Yes, the description is about right, as far as it goes. But the Cricket is still waiting for the few lines needed to bring his merits before the public; and since La Fontaine neglected him, he will have to go on waiting a long time.

To me, as a naturalist, the important point in the two fables is the burrow on which the moral is founded. Florian speaks of the

---

[1]English translation by Mr. Stephen M'Kenna.

snug retreat; the other praises his lowly home. It is the dwelling, therefore, that above all compels attention, even that of the poet, who as a rule cares little for realities.

In this matter, indeed, the Cricket is extraordinary. Of all our insects he is the only one who, when full-grown, possesses a fixed home, the reward of his own industry. During the bad season of the year, most of the others burrow or skulk in some temporary refuge, a refuge obtained free of cost and abandoned without regret. Several of them create marvels with a view to settling their family: cotton satchels, baskets made of leaves, towers of cement. Some live permanently in ambush, lying in wait for their prey. The Tiger-beetle, for instance, digs himself a perpendicular hole, which he stops up with his flat, bronze head. If any other insect steps on this deceptive trap-door it immediately tips up, and the unhappy wayfarer disappears into the gulf. The Ant-lion makes a slanting funnel in the sand. Its victim, the Ant, slides down the slant and is then stoned, from the bottom of the funnel, by the hunter, who turns his neck into a catapult. But these are all temporary refuges or traps.

The laboriously constructed home, in which the insect settles down with no intention of moving, either in the happy spring or in the woeful winter season; the real manor-house, built for peace and comfort, and not as a hunting-box or a nursery—this is known to the Cricket alone. On some sunny, grassy slope he is the owner of a hermitage. While all the others lead vagabond lives, sleeping in the open air or under the casual shelter of a dead leaf or a stone, or the peeling bark of an old tree, he is a privileged person with a permanent address.

The making of a home is a serious problem. It has been solved by the Cricket, by the Rabbit, and lastly by man. In my neighbourhood the Fox and the Badger have holes, which are largely formed by the irregularities of the rock. A few repairs, and the dug-out is completed. The Rabbit is cleverer than these, for he builds his house by burrowing wherever he pleases, when there is no natural passage that allows him to settle down free of all trouble.

The Cricket is cleverer than any of them. He scorns chance refuges, and always chooses the site of his home carefully, in well-drained ground, with a pleasant sunny aspect. He refuses to make use of ready-made caves that are inconvenient and rough: he digs every bit of his villa, from the entrance-hall to the back-room.

I see no one above him, in the art of house-building, except man; and even man, before mixing mortar to hold stones together, or kneading clay to coat his hut of branches, fought with wild beasts for a refuge in the rocks. Why is it that a special instinct is bestowed on one particular creature? Here is one of the humblest of creatures able to lodge himself to perfection. He has a home, an advantage unknown to many civilised beings; he has a peaceful retreat, the first condition of comfort; and no one around him is capable of settling down. He has no rivals but ourselves.

Whence does he derive this gift? Is he favoured with special tools? No, the Cricket is not an expert in the art of digging; in fact, one is rather surprised at the result when one considers the feebleness of his means.

Is a home a necessity to him, on account of an exceptionally delicate skin? No, his near kinsmen have skins as sensitive as his, yet do not dread the open air at all.

Is the house-building talent the result of his anatomy? Has he any special organ that suggests it? No: in my neighbourhood there are three other Crickets who are so much like the Field Cricket in appearance, colour, and structure, that at the first glance one would take them for him. Of these faithful copies, not one knows how to dig himself a burrow. The Double-spotted Cricket inhabits the heaps of grass that are left to rot in damp places; the Solitary Cricket roams about the dry clods turned up by the gardener's spade; the Bordeaux Cricket is not afraid to make his way into our houses, where he sings discreetly, during August and September, in some cool, dark spot.

There is no object in continuing these questions: the answer would always be No. Instinct never tells us its causes. It depends so little on an insect's stock of tools that no detail of anatomy, nothing in the creature's formation, can explain it to us or make us foresee it. These four similar Crickets, of whom only one can burrow, are enough to show us our ignorance of the origin of instinct.

Who does not know the Cricket's house? Who has not, as a child playing in the fields, stopped in front of the hermit's cabin? However light your footfall, he has heard you coming, and has abruptly withdrawn to the very bottom of his hiding-place. When you arrive, the threshold of the house is deserted.

Every one knows the way to bring out the skulker. You insert a straw and move it gently about the burrow. Surprised at what is happening above, the tickled and teased Cricket ascends from his back room; he stops in the passage, hesitates, and waves his delicate antennæ inquiringly. He comes to the light, and, once outside, he is easy to catch, since these events have puzzled his poor head. Should he be missed at the first attempt he may become suspicious and refuse to appear. In that case he can be flooded out with a glass of water.

Those were adorable times when we were children, and hunted Crickets along the grassy paths, and put them in cages, and fed them on a leaf of lettuce. They all come back to me to-day, those times, as I search the burrows for subjects to study. They seem like yesterday when my companion, little Paul, an expert in the use of the straw, springs up suddenly after a long trial of skill and patience, and cries excitedly: "I've got him! I've got him!"

Quick, here's a bag! In you go, my little Cricket! You shall be petted and pampered, but you must teach us something, and first of all you must show us your house.

II

His House

It is a slanting gallery in the grass, on some sunny bank which soon dries after a shower. It is nine inches long at most, hardly as thick as one's finger, and straight or bent according to the nature of the ground. As a rule, a tuft of grass half conceals the home, serving as a porch and throwing the entrance discreetly into shadow. When the Cricket goes out to browse upon the surrounding turf he does not touch this turf. The gently sloping threshold, carefully raked and swept, extends for some distance;

and this is the terrace on which, when everything is peaceful round about, the Cricket sits and scrapes his fiddle.

The inside of the house is devoid of luxury, with bare and yet not coarse walls. The inhabitant has plenty of leisure to do away with any unpleasant roughness. At the end of the passage is the bedroom, a little more carefully smoothed than the rest, and slightly wider. All said, it is a very simple abode, exceedingly clean, free from damp, and conforming to the rules of hygiene. On the other hand, it is an enormous undertaking, a gigantic tunnel, when we consider the modest tools with which the Cricket has to dig. If we wish to know how he does it, and when he sets to work, we must go back to the time when the egg is laid.

The Cricket lays her eggs singly in the soil, like the Decticus, at a depth of three-quarters of an inch. She arranges them in groups, and lays altogether about five or six hundred. The egg is a little marvel of mechanism. After the hatching it appears as an opaque white cylinder, with a round and very regular hole at the top. To the edge of this hole is fastened a cap, like a lid. Instead of bursting open anyhow under the thrusts of the larva within, it opens of its own accord along a circular line—a specially prepared line of least resistance.

About a fortnight after the egg is laid, two large, round, rusty-black dots darken the front end. A little way above these two dots, right at the top of the cylinder, you see the outline of a thin circular swelling. This is the line where the shell is preparing to break open. Soon the transparency of the egg allows one to see the delicate markings of the tiny creature's segments. Now is the time to be on the watch, especially in the morning.

Fortune loves the persevering, and if we pay constant visits to the eggs we shall be rewarded. All round the swelling, where the resistance of the shell has gradually been overcome, the end of the egg becomes detached. Being pushed back by the forehead of the little creature within, it rises and falls to one side like the top of a tiny scent-bottle. The Cricket pops out like a Jack-in-the-box.

When he is gone the shell remains distended, smooth, intact, pure white, with the cap or lid hanging from the opening. A bird's egg breaks clumsily under the blows of a wart that grows for the purpose at the end of the Chick's beak; the Cricket's egg is more ingeniously made, and opens like an ivory case. The thrust of the creature's head is enough to work the hinge.

I said above that, when the lid is lifted, a young Cricket pops out; but this is not quite accurate. What appears is the swaddled grub, as yet unrecognisable in a tight-fitting sheath. The Decticus, you will remember, who is hatched in the same way under the soil, wears a protective covering during his journey to the surface. The Cricket is related to the Decticus, and therefore wears the same livery, although in point of fact he does not need it. The egg of the Decticus remains underground for eight months, so the poor grub has to fight its way through soil that has grown hard, and it therefore needs a covering for its long shanks. But the Cricket is shorter and stouter, and since its egg is only in the ground for a few days it has nothing worse than a powdery layer of earth to pass through. For these reasons it requires no overall, and leaves it behind in the shell.

As soon as he is rid of his swaddling-clothes the young Cricket, pale all over, almost white, begins to battle with the soil overhead. He hits out with his mandibles; he sweeps aside and kicks behind him the powdery earth, which offers no resistance. Very soon he is on the surface, amidst the joys of the sunlight and the perils of conflict with his fellow-creatures—poor feeble mite that he is, hardly larger than a Flea.

By the end of twenty-four hours he has turned into a magnificent blackamoor, whose ebon hue vies with that of the full-grown insect. All that remains of his original pallor is a white sash that girds his chest. Very nimble and alert, he sounds the surrounding air with his long, quivering antennæ, and runs and jumps about with great impetuosity. Some day he will be too fat to indulge in such antics.

And now we see why the mother Cricket lays so many eggs. It is because most of the young ones are doomed to death. They are massacred in huge numbers by other insects, and especially by the little Grey Lizard and the Ant. The latter, loathsome free-booter that she is, hardly leaves me a Cricket in my garden. She snaps up the poor little creatures and gobbles them down at frantic speed.

Oh, the execrable wretch! And to think that we place the Ant in the front rank of insects! Books are written in her honour, and the stream of praise never runs dry. The naturalists hold her in great esteem; and add daily to her fame. It would seem that with animals, as with men, the surest way to attract attention is to do harm to others.

Nobody asks about the Beetles who do such valuable work as scavengers, whereas everybody knows the Gnat, that drinker of men's blood; the Wasp, that hot-tempered swashbuckler, with her poisoned dagger; and the Ant, that notorious evil-doer who, in our southern villages, saps and imperils the rafters of a dwelling as cheerfully as she eats a fig.

The Ant massacres the Crickets in my garden so thoroughly that I am driven to look for them outside the enclosure. In August, among the fallen leaves, where the grass has not been wholly scorched by the sun, I find the young Cricket, already rather big, and now black all over, with not a vestige of his white girdle remaining. At this period of his life he is a vagabond: the shelter of a dead leaf or a flat stone is enough for him.

Many of those who survived the raids of the Ants now fall victims to the Wasp, who hunts down the wanderers and stores them underground. If they would but dig their dwellings a few weeks before the usual time they would be saved; but they never think of it. They are faithful to their ancient customs.

It is at the close of October, when the first cold weather threatens, that the burrow is taken in hand. The work is very simple, if I may judge by my observation of the caged insect. The digging is never done at a bare point in the pan, but always under the shelter of some withered lettuce-leaf, a remnant of the food provided. This takes the place of the grass tuft that seems indispensable to the secrecy of the home.

The miner scrapes with his fore-legs, and uses the pincers of his mandibles to pull out the larger bits of gravel. I see him stamping with his powerful hind-legs, furnished with a double row of spikes; I see him raking the rubbish, sweeping it backwards and spreading it slantwise. There you have the whole process.

The work proceeds pretty quickly at first. In the yielding soil of my cages the digger disappears underground after a spell that lasts a couple of hours. He returns to the entrance at intervals, always backwards and always sweeping. Should he be overcome with fatigue he takes a rest on the threshold of his half-finished home, with his head outside and his antennæ waving feebly. He goes in again, and resumes work with pinchers and rakes. Soon the periods of rest become longer, and wear out my patience.

The most urgent part of the work is done. Once the hole is a couple of inches deep, it suffices for the needs of the moment. The rest will be a long affair, carried out in a leisurely way, a little one day and a little the next: the hole will be made deeper and wider as the weather grows colder and the insect larger. Even in winter, if the temperature be mild and the sun shining on the entrance to the dwelling, it is not unusual to see the Cricket shooting out rubbish. Amid the joys of spring the upkeep of the building still continues. It is constantly undergoing improvements and repairs until the owner's death.

When April ends the Cricket's song begins; at first in rare and shy solos, but soon in a general symphony in which each clod of turf boasts its performer. I am more than inclined to place the Cricket at the head of the spring choristers. In our waste-lands, when the thyme and lavender are gaily flowering, the Crested Lark rises like a lyrical rocket, his throat swelling with notes, and from the sky sheds his sweet music upon the fallows. Down below the Crickets chant the responses. Their song is monotonous and artless, but well suited in its very lack of art to the simple gladness of reviving life. It is the hosanna of the awakening, the sacred alleluia understood by swelling seed and sprouting blade. In this duet I should award the palm to the Cricket. His numbers and his unceasing note deserve it. Were the Lark to fall silent, the fields blue-grey with lavender, swinging its fragrant censors before the sun, would still receive from this humble chorister a solemn hymn of praise.

III

His Musical-Box

In steps Science, and says to the Cricket bluntly: "Show us your musical-box."

Like all things of real value, it is very simple. It is based on the same principle as that of the Grasshoppers: a bow with a hook to it, and a vibrating membrane. The right wing-case overlaps the left and covers it almost completely, except where it folds back sharply and encases the insect's side. It is the opposite arrangement to that which we find in the Green Grasshopper, the Decticus, and their kinsmen. The Cricket is right-handed, the others left-handed.

The two wing-cases are made in exactly the same way. To know one is to know the other. They lie flat on the insect's back, and slant suddenly at the side in a right-angled fold, encircling the body with a delicately veined pinion.

If you hold one of these wing-cases up to the light you will see that it is a very pale red, save for two large adjoining spaces; a larger, triangular one in front, and a smaller, oval one at the back. They are crossed by faint wrinkles. These two spaces are the sounding-boards, or drums. The skin is finer here than elsewhere, and transparent, though of a somewhat smoky tint.

At the hinder edge of the front part are two curved, parallel veins, with a cavity between them. This cavity contains five or six little black wrinkles that look like the rungs of a tiny ladder. They supply friction: they intensify the vibration by increasing the number of points touched by the bow.

On the lower surface one of the two veins that surround the cavity of the rungs becomes a rib cut into the shape of a hook. This is the bow. It is provided with about a hundred and fifty triangular teeth of exquisite geometrical regularity.

It is a fine instrument indeed. The hundred and fifty teeth of the bow, biting into the rungs of the opposite wing-case, set the four drums in motion at one and the same time, the lower pair by direct friction, the upper pair by the shaking of the friction-apparatus. What a rush of sound! The Cricket with his four drums throws his music to a distance of some hundreds of yards.

He vies with the Cicada in shrillness, without having the latter's disagreeable harshness. And better still: this favoured creature knows how to modulate his song. The wing-cases, as I said, extend over each side in a wide fold. These are the dampers which, lowered to a greater or less depth, alter the intensity of the sound. According to the extent of their contact with the soft body of the Cricket they allow him to sing gently at one time and *fortissimo* at another.

The exact similarity of the two wing-cases is worthy of attention. I can see clearly the function of the upper bow, and the four sounding-spaces which sets it in motion; but what is the good of the lower one, the bow on the left wing? Not resting on anything, it has nothing to strike with its hook, which is as carefully toothed as the other. It is absolutely useless, unless the apparatus can invert the order of its two parts, and place that above which is below. If that could be done, the perfect symmetry of the instrument is such that the mechanism would be the same as before, and the insect would be able to play with the bow that is at present useless. The lower fiddlestick would become the upper, and the tune would be the same.

I suspected at first that the Cricket could use both bows, or at least that there were some who were permanently left-handed. But observation has convinced me of the contrary. All the Crickets I have examined—and they are many—without a single exception carried the right wing-case above the left.

I even tried to bring about by artificial means what Nature refused to show me. Using my forceps, very gently of course, and without straining the wing-cases, I made these overlap the opposite way. It is easily done with a little skill and patience. Everything went well: there was no dislocation of the shoulders, the membranes were not creased.

I almost expected the Cricket to sing, but I was soon undeceived. He submitted for a few moments; but then, finding himself uncomfortable, he made an effort and restored his instrument to its usual position. In vain I repeated the operation: the Cricket's obstinacy triumphed over mine.

Then I thought I would make the attempt while the wing-cases were quite new and plastic, at the moment when the larva casts its skin. I secured one at the point of being transformed. At this stage the future wings and wing-cases form four tiny flaps, which, by their shape and scantiness, and by the way they stick out in different directions, remind me of the short jackets worn by the Auvergne cheesemakers. The larva cast off these garments before my eyes.

The wing-cases developed bit by bit, and opened out. There was no sign to tell me which would overlap the other. Then the edges touched: a few moments longer and the right would be over the left. This was the time to intervene.

With a straw I gently changed the position, bringing the left edge over the right. In spite of some protest from the insect I was quite successful: the left wing-case pushed forward, though only very little. Then I left it alone, and gradually the wing-cases matured in the inverted position. The Cricket was left-handed. I expected soon to see him wield the fiddlestick which the members of his family never employ.

On the third day he made a start. A few brief grating sounds were heard—the noise of a machine out of gear shifting its parts back into their proper order. Then the tune began, with its accustomed tone and rhythm.

Alas, I had been over-confident in my mischievous straw! I thought I had created a new type of instrumentalist, and I had obtained nothing at all! The Cricket was scraping with his right fiddlestick, and always would. With a painful effort he had dislocated his shoulders, which I had forced to harden in the wrong way. He had put back on top that which ought to be on top, and underneath that which ought to be underneath. My sorry science tried to make a left-handed player of him. He laughed at my devices, and settled down to be right-handed for the rest of his life.

Enough of the instrument; let us listen to the music. The Cricket sings on the threshold of his house, in the cheerful sunshine, never indoors. The wing-cases utter their *cri-cri* in a soft *tremolo*. It is full, sonorous, nicely cadenced, and lasts indefinitely. Thus are the leisures of solitude beguiled all through the spring. The hermit at first sings for his own pleasure. Glad to be alive, he chants the praises of the sun that shines upon him, the grass that feeds him, the peaceful retreat that harbours him. The first object of his bow is to hymn the pleasures of life.

Later on he plays to his mate. But, to tell the truth, his attention is rewarded with little gratitude; for in the end she quarrels with him ferociously, and unless he takes to flight she cripples him—and even eats him more or less. But indeed, in any case he soon dies. Even if he escapes his pugnacious mate, he perishes in June. We are told that the music-loving Greeks used to keep Cicadæ in cages, the better to enjoy their singing. I venture to disbelieve the story. In the first place the harsh clicking of the Cicadæ, when long continued at close quarters, is a torture to ears that are at all delicate. The Greeks' sense of hearing was too well trained to take pleasure in such raucous sounds away from the general concert of the fields, which is heard at a distance.

In the second place it is absolutely impossible to bring up Cicadæ in captivity, unless we cover over a whole olive-tree or plane-tree. A single day spent in a cramped enclosure would make the high-flying insect die of boredom.

Is it not possible that people have confused the Cricket with the Cicada, as they also do the Green Grasshopper? With the Cricket they would be quite right. He is one who bears captivity gaily: his stay-at-home ways predispose him to it. He lives happily and whirrs without ceasing in a cage no larger than a man's fist, provided that he has his lettuce-leaf every day. Was it not he whom the small boys of Athens reared in little wire cages hanging on a window-frame?

The small boys of Provence, and all the South, have the same tastes. In the towns a Cricket becomes the child's treasured possession. The insect, petted and pampered, sings to him of the simple joys of the country. Its death throws the whole household into a sort of mourning.

The three other Crickets of my neighbourhood all carry the same musical instrument as the Field Cricket, with slight variation of detail. Their song is much alike in all cases, allowing for differences of size. The smallest of the family, the Bordeaux Cricket, sometimes ventures into the dark corners of my kitchen, but his song is so faint that it takes a very attentive ear to hear it.

The Field Cricket sings during the sunniest hours of the spring: during the still summer nights we have the Italian Cricket. He is a slender, feeble insect, quite pale, almost white, as beseems his nocturnal habits. You are afraid of crushing him, if you so much as take him in your fingers. He lives high in air, on shrubs of every kind, or on the taller grasses; and he rarely descends to earth. His song, the sweet music of the still, hot evenings from July to October, begins at sunset and continues for the best part of the night.

This song is known to everybody here in Provence, for the smallest clump of bushes has its orchestra. The soft, slow *gri-i-i gri-i-i* is made more expressive by a slight *tremolo*. If nothing happens to disturb the insect the sound remains unaltered; but at the least noise the musician becomes a ventriloquist. You hear him quite close, in front of you; and then, all of a sudden, you hear him fifteen yards away. You move towards the sound. It is not there: it comes from the original place. No, it doesn't after all. Is it over there on the left, or does it come from behind? One is absolutely at a loss, quite unable to find the spot where the music is chirping.

This illusion of varying distance is produced in two ways. The sounds become loud or soft, open or muffled, according to the exact part of the lower wing-case that is pressed by the bow. And they are also modified by the position of the wing-cases. For the loud sounds these are raised to their full height: for the muffled sounds they are lowered more or less. The pale Cricket misleads those who hunt for him by pressing the edges of his vibrating flaps against his soft body.

I know no prettier or more limpid insect-song than his, heard in the deep stillness of an August evening. How often have I lain down on the ground among the rosemary bushes of my *harmas,* to listen to the delightful concert!

The Italian Cricket swarms in my enclosure. Every tuft of red-flowering rock-rose has its chorister; so has every clump of lavender. The bushy arbutus-shrubs, the turpentine-trees, all become orchestras. And in its clear voice, so full of charm, the whole of this little world, from every shrub and every branch, sings of the gladness of life.

High up above my head the Swan stretches its great cross along the Milky Way: below, all round me, the insect's symphony rises and falls. Infinitesimal life telling its joys makes me forget the pageant of the stars. Those celestial eyes look down upon me, placid and cold, but do not stir a fibre within me. Why? They lack the great secret—life. Our reason tells us, it is true, that those suns warm worlds like ours; but when all is said, this belief is no more than a guess, it is not a certainty.

In your company, on the contrary, O my Cricket, I feel the throbbing of life, which is the soul of our lump of clay; and that is why, under my rosemary-hedge, I give but an absent glance at the constellation of the Swan and devote all my attention to your serenade! A living speck—the merest dab of life—capable of pleasure and pain, is far more interesting to me than all the immensities of mere matter.

CHAPTER XIII

The Sisyphus

You are not tired, I hope, of hearing about the Scavenger Beetles with a talent for making balls. I have told you of the Sacred Beetle and of the Spanish Copris, and now I wish to say a few words of yet another of these creatures. In the insect world we meet with a great many model mothers: it is only fair, for once to draw attention to a good father.

Now a good father is rarely seen except among the higher animals. The bird is excellent in this respect, and the furred folk perform their duties honourably. Lower in the scale of living creatures the father is generally indifferent to his family. Very few insects are exceptions to this rule. This heartlessness, which would be detestable in the higher ranks of the animal kingdom, where the weakness of the young demands prolonged care, is excusable among insect fathers. For the robustness of the new-born insect enables it to gather its food unaided, provided it be in a suitable place. When all that the Pieris need do for the safety of the race is to lay her eggs on the leaves of a cabbage, of what use would a father's care be? The mother's botanical instinct needs no assistance. At laying-time the other parent would be in the way.

Most insects adopt this simple method of upbringing. They merely choose a dining-room which will be the home of the family once it is hatched, or else a place that will allow the young ones to find suitable fare for themselves. There is no need for the father in such cases. He generally dies without lending the least assistance in the work of setting up his offspring in life.

Things do not always happen, however, in quite such a primitive fashion. There are tribes that provide a dowry for their families, that prepare board and lodging for them in advance. The Bees and Wasps in particular are masters in the industry of making cellars, jars, and satchels, in which the ration of honey is hoarded: they are perfect in the art of creating burrows stocked with the game that forms the food of their grubs.

Well, this enormous labour, which is one of building and provisioning combined, this toil in which the insect's whole life is spent, is done by the mother alone. It wears her out; it utterly exhausts her. The father drunk with sunlight, stands idle at the edge of the workyard, watching his plucky helpmate at her job.

Why does he not lend the mother a helping hand? It is now or never. Why does he not follow the example of the Swallow couple, both of whom bring their bit of straw, their blob of mortar to the building and their Midge to the young ones? He does nothing of the kind. Possibly he puts forward his comparative weakness as an excuse. It is a poor argument; for to cut a disk out of a leaf, to scrape some cotton from a downy plant, to collect a little bit of cement in muddy places would not overtax his strength. He could very easily help, at any rate as a labourer; he is quite fit to gather materials for the mother, with her greater intelligence, to fit in place. The real reason of his inactivity is sheer incapability.

It is strange that the most gifted of the industrial insects should know nothing of a father's duties. One would expect the highest talents to be developed in him by the needs of the young; but he remains as dull-witted as a Butterfly, whose family is reared at so small a cost. We are baffled at every turn by the question: Why is a particular instinct given to one insect and denied to another?

It baffles us so thoroughly that we are extremely surprised when we find in the scavenger the noble qualities that are denied to the honey-gatherer. Various Scavenger Beetles are accustomed to help in the burden of housekeeping, and know the value of working in double harness. The Geotrupes couple, for instance, prepare their larva's food together: the father lends his mate the assistance of his powerful press in the manufacture of the tightly packed sausage-shaped ration. He is a splendid example of domestic habits, and one extremely surprising amid the general egoism.

To this example my constant studies of the subject have enabled me to add three others, all furnished by the Guild of Scavengers.

One of them is the Sisyphus, the smallest and most zealous of all our pill-rollers. He is the liveliest and most agile of them all, and recks nothing of awkward somersaults and headlong falls on the impossible roads to which his obstinacy brings him back again and again. It was in reference to these wild gymnastics that Latreille gave him the name of Sisyphus.

As you know, that unhappy wretch of classical fame had a terrible task. He was forced to roll a huge stone uphill; and each time he succeeded in toiling to the top of the mountain the stone slipped from his grasp and rolled to the bottom. I like this myth. It is the history of a good many of us. So far as I am concerned, for half a century and more I have painfully climbed the steep ascent, spending my strength recklessly in the struggle to hoist up to safety that crushing burden, my daily bread. Hardly is the loaf balanced when it slips off, slides down, and is lost in the abyss.

The Sisyphus with whom we are now concerned knows none of these bitter trials. Untroubled by the steep slopes he gaily trundles his load, at one time bread for himself, at another bread for his children. He is very scarce in these parts; and I should never have managed to secure a suitable number of subjects for my studies had it not been for an assistant whom I have already mentioned more than once.

I speak of my little son Paul, aged seven. He is my enthusiastic companion on my hunting expeditions, and knows better than any one of his age the secrets of the Cicada, the Locust, the Cricket, and especially the Scavenger Beetle. Twenty paces away his sharp eyes will distinguish the real mound that marks a burrow from casual heaps of earth. His delicate ears catch the Grasshopper's faint song, which is quite unheard by me. He lends me his sight and hearing; and I, in exchange, present him with ideas, which he receives attentively.

Little Paul has his own insect-cages, in which the Sacred

Beetle makes pears for him; his own little garden, no larger than a pocket-handkerchief, where he grows beans, often digging them up to see if the tiny roots are any longer; his forest planta- tion, in which stand four oaks a hand's-breadth high, still fur- nished on one side with the acorn that feeds them. It all makes a welcome change from grammar, which gets on none the worse for it.

When the month of May is near at hand Paul and I get up early one morning—so early that we start without our break- fast—and we explore, at the foot of the mountain, the meadows where the flocks have been. Here we find the Sisyphus. Paul is so zealous in his search that we soon have a sufficient number of couples.

All that is needed for their well-being is a wire-gauze cover, with a bed of sand and a supply of their food—to obtain which we too turn scavengers. These creatures are so small, hardly the size of a cherry-stone! And so curious in shape withal! A dumpy body, the hinder end of which is pointed, and very long legs, resembling a Spider's when outspread. The hind-legs are of amazing length, and are curved, which is most useful for clasp- ing and squeezing the pellet.

Soon the time comes for establishing the family. With equal zeal father and mother alike take part in kneading, carting, and stowing away the provisions for the young ones. With the cleaver of the fore-legs a morsel of the right size is cut from the food placed at their disposal. The two insects work at the piece together, giving it little pats, pressing it, and shaping it into a ball as large as a big pea.

As in the Sacred Beetle's workshop, the accurately round shape is obtained without the mechanical trick of rolling the ball. The material is modelled into a sphere before it is moved, before it is even loosened from its support. Here, once more, we have an expert in geometry familiar with the best form for pre- serving food.

The ball is soon ready. It must now, by vigorous rolling, be given the crust which will protect the soft stuff within from becoming too dry. The mother, who can be recognised by her slightly larger size, harnesses herself in the place of honour, in

front. With her long hind-legs on the ground, and her fore-legs
on the ball, she hauls it towards her, backwards. The father
pushes behind in the reverse position, head downwards. It is
precisely the same method as that of the Sacred Beetle when
working in twos, but it has another object. The Sisyphus team
conveys a store of food for the grubs, whereas the big pill-rollers
trundle a banquet which they themselves will eat up underground.

The couple start off along the ground. They have no definite
goal, but walk in a direct line, without regard to the obstacles
that lie in the way. In this backward march the obstacles could
not be avoided; but even if they were seen the Sisyphus would
not try to go round them. For she even makes obstinate
attempts to climb the wire-work of my cage. This is an arduous
and impossible task. Clawing the meshes of the gauze with her
hind-legs the mother pulls the load towards her; then, putting
her fore-legs round it, she holds it suspended in air. The father,
finding nothing to stand upon, clings to the ball—encrusts himself in it, so to speak, thus adding his weight to that of the lump,
and taking no further pains. The effort is too great to last. The
ball and its rider, forming one mass, fall to the floor. The mother, from above, looks down for a moment in surprise, and then
drops to recover the load and renew her impossible attempt to
scale the side. After repeated falls the climb is abandoned.

Even on level ground the carting is not carried on without difficulty. At every moment the load swerves on some mound
made by a bit of gravel; and the team topple over and kick
about, upside down. This is a trifle, the merest trifle. These
tumbles, which so often fling the Sisyphus on his back, cause
him no concern; one would even think he liked them. After all,
the ball has to be hardened and made of the right consistency.
And this being the case, bumps, falls, and jolts are all part of the
programme. This mad steeple-chasing goes on for hours.

At last the mother, regarding the work as completed, goes off
a little way in search of a suitable spot. The father mounts guard,
squatting on the treasure. If his companion's absence be unduly
long, he relieves his boredom by spinning the ball nimbly
between his uplifted hind legs. He treats his precious pellet as a

juggler treats his ball. He tests its perfect shape with his curved legs, the branches of his compasses. No one who sees him frisking in that jubilant attitude can doubt his lively satisfaction—the satisfaction of a father assured of his children's future.

"It is I," he seems to say, "I who kneaded this round loaf, I who made this bread for my sons!"

And he lifts on high, for all to see, this magnificent testimony to his industry.

Meanwhile the mother has chosen a site for the burrow. A shallow pit is made, a mere beginning of the work. The ball is rolled near it. The father, that vigilant guardian, does not let go, while the mother digs with her legs and forehead. Soon the hollow is big enough to hold the pellet. She insists on having it quite close to her; she must feel it bobbing up and down behind her, on her back, safe from parasites, before she decides to go farther. She is afraid of what might happen to it if it were left on the edge of the burrow until the home were completed. There are plenty of Midges and other such insects to grab it. One cannot be too careful.

The ball therefore is inserted, half in and half out of the partly-formed basin. The mother, underneath, gets her legs round it and pulls: the father above, lets it down gently, and sees that the hole is not choked up with falling earth. All goes well. The digging is resumed and the descent continues, always with the same caution; one of the insects pulling the load, the other regulating the drop and clearing away anything that might hinder the operation. A few more efforts, and the ball disappears underground with the two miners. What follows for some time to come can only be a repetition of what has already been done. We must wait half a day or so.

If we keep careful watch we shall see the father come up again to the surface by himself, and crouch in the sand near the burrow. Detained below by duties in which her companion can be of no assistance to her, the mother usually postpones her appearance till the morrow. At last she shows herself. The father leaves the place where he was snoozing, and joins her. The reunited couple go back to the spot where their food-stuffs are to be found, and having refreshed themselves they gather up more materials. The two then set to work again. Once more they model, cart, and store the ball together.

I am delighted with this constancy. That it is really the rule I dare not declare. There must, no doubt, be flighty, fickle Beetles. No matter: the little I have seen gives me a high opinion of the domestic habits of the Sisyphus.

It is time to inspect the burrow. At no great depth we find a tiny niche, just large enough to allow the mother to move round her work. The smallness of the chamber tells us that the father cannot remain there for long. When the studio is ready, he must go away to leave the sculptress room to turn.

The contents of the cellar consist of a single ball, a masterpiece of art. It is a copy of the Sacred Beetle's pear on a very much reduced scale, its smallness making the polish of the surface and the elegance of the curves all the more striking. Its diameter, at the broadest point, measures one-half to three-quarters of an inch.

One more observation about the Sisyphus. Six couples under the wire-gauze cover gave me fifty-seven pears containing one egg each—an average of over nine grubs to each couple. The Sacred Beetle is far from reaching this figure. To what cause are we to attribute this large brood? I can see but one: the fact that the father works as well as the mother. Family burdens that would exceed the strength of one are not too heavy when there are two to bear them.

CHAPTER XIV

The Capricorn

I

The Grub's Home

An eighteenth-century philosopher, Condillac, describes an imaginary statue, organised like a man, but with none of a man's senses. He then pictures the effect of endowing it with the five senses, one by one, and the first sense he gives it is that of smell. The statue, having no sense but smell, inhales the scent of a rose, and out of that single impression creates a whole world of ideas. In my youth I owed some happy moments to that statue. I seemed to see it come to life in that action of the nostrils, acquiring memory, concentration, judgment, and other mental qualities, even as still waters are aroused and rippled by the impact of a grain of sand. I recovered from my illusion under the teaching of my abler master the animal. The Capricorn taught me that the problem is more obscure than the Abbé Condillac led me to suppose.

When my winter supply of firewood is being prepared for me with wedge and mallet, the woodman selects, by my express orders, the oldest and most ravaged trunks in his stack. My tastes bring a smile to his lips; he wonders by what whimsy I prefer wood that is worm-eaten to sound wood, which burns so much better. I have my views on the subject, and the worthy man submits to them.

A fine oak-trunk, seamed with scars and gashed with wounds, contains many treasures for my studies. The mallet drives home, the wedges bite, the wood splits; and within, in the dry and hollow parts, are revealed groups of various insects who are capable of living through the cold season, and have here taken up their winter quarters. In the low-roofed galleries built by some

Beetle, the Osmia Bee has piled her cells one above the other. In the deserted chambers and vestibules Megachiles have arranged their leafy jars. In the live wood, filled with juicy sap, the larva of the Capricorn, the chief author of the oak's undoing, has set up its home.

Truly they are strange creatures, these grubs: bits of intestines crawling about! In the middle of Autumn I find them of two different ages. The older are almost as thick as one's finger; the others hardly attain the diameter of a pencil. I find, in addition, the pupa or nymph more or less fully coloured, and the perfect insect ready to leave the trunk when the hot weather comes again. Life inside the wood, therefore, lasts for three years.

How is this long period of solitude and captivity spent? In wandering lazily through the thickness of the oak, in making roads whose rubbish serves as food. The horse in the book of Job "swallows the ground" in a figure of speech: the Capricorn's grub eats its way literally. With its carpenter's-gouge—a strong black mandible, short and without notches, but scooped into a sharp-edged spoon—it digs the opening of its tunnel. From the piece cut out the grub extracts the scanty juices, while the refuse accumulates behind him in heaps. The path is devoured as it is made; it is blocked behind as it makes way ahead.

Since this harsh work is done with the two gouges, the two curved chisels of the mandibles, the Capricorn-grub requires much strength in the front part of its body, which therefore swells into a sort of pestle. The Buprestis-grub, that other industrious carpenter, adopts a similar form, and even exaggerates its pestle. The part that toils and carves hard wood requires to be robust; the rest of the body, which has but to follow after, continues slim. The essential thing is that the implement of the jaws should possess a solid support and powerful machinery. The Capricorn larva strengthens its chisels with a stout, black, horny armour that surrounds the mouth; yet, apart from its skull and its equipment of tools, this grub has a skin as fine as satin and as white as ivory. This dead white is caused by a thick layer of grease, which one would not expect a diet of wood to produce in the animal. True, it has nothing to do, at every hour of the day and night, but gnaw. The quantity of wood that passes into its stomach makes up for the lack of nourishing qualities.

The grub's legs can hardly be called legs at all; they are mere suggestions of the legs the full-grown insect will have by and by. They are infinitesimal in size, and of no use whatever for walking. They do not even touch the supporting surface, being kept off it by the plumpness of the chest. The organs by means of which the animal progresses are something altogether different.

The grub of the Rose-chafer, with the aid of the hairs and pad-like projections upon its spine, manages to reverse the usual method of walking, and to wriggle along on its back. The grub of the Capricorn is even more ingenious: it moves at the same time on its back and its stomach. To take the place of its useless legs it has a walking apparatus almost like feet, which appear, contrary to every rule, on the surface of its back.

On the middle part of its body, both above and below, there is a row of seven four-sided pads, which the grub can either expand or contract, making them stick out or lie flat at will. It is by means of these pads that it walks. When it wishes to move forward it expands the hinder pads, those on the back as well as those on the stomach, and contracts its front pads. The swelling of the hind pads in the narrow gallery fills up the space, and gives the grub something to push against. At the same time the flattening of the front pads, by decreasing the size of the grub, allows it to slip forward and take half a step. Then, to complete the step, the hind-quarters must be brought up the same distance. With this object the front pads fill out and provide support, while those behind shrink and leave room for the grub to draw up its hind-quarters.

With the double support of its back and stomach, with alternate swellings and shrinkings, the animal easily advances or retreats along its gallery, a sort of mould which the contents fill without a gap. But if the pads grip only on one side progress becomes impossible. When placed on the smooth wood of my table the animal wriggles slowly; it lengthens and shortens without progressing by a hair's breadth. Laid on the surface of a piece of split oak, a rough, uneven surface due to the gash made by the wedge, it twists and writhes, moves the front part of its body very slowly from left to right and right to left, lifts it a little, lowers it, and begins again. This is all it can do. The rudimentary legs remain inert and absolutely useless.

II

The Grub's Sensations

Though the Capricorn-grub possesses these useless legs, the germs of future limbs, there is no sign of the eyes with which the fully-developed insect will be richly gifted. The larva has not the least trace of any organs of sight. What would it do with sight, in the murky thickness of a tree-trunk? Hearing is likewise absent. In the untroubled silence of the oak's inmost heart the sense of hearing would be superfluous. Where sounds are lacking, of what use is the faculty of discerning them?

To make the matter certain I carried out some experiments. If split lengthwise the grub's abode becomes a half-tunnel, in which I can watch the occupant's doings. When left alone it alternately works for a while, gnawing at its gallery, and rests for awhile, fixed by its pads to the two sides of the tunnel. I took advantage of these moments of rest to inquire into its power of hearing. The banging of hard bodies, the ring of metallic objects, the grating of a file upon a saw, were tried in vain. The animal remained impassive: not a wince, not a movement of the skin, no sign of awakened attention. I succeeded no better when I scratched the wood near it with a hard point, to imitate the sound of some other grub at work in its neighbourhood. The indifference to my noisy tricks could be no greater in a lifeless object. The animal is deaf.

Can it smell? Everything tells us that it cannot. Scent is of assistance in the search for food. But the Capricorn-grub need not go in quest of eatables. It feeds on its home; it lives on the wood that gives it shelter. Nevertheless I tested it. In a log of fresh cypress wood I made a groove of the same width as that of the natural galleries, and I placed the grub inside it. Cypress wood is strongly scented; it has the smell characteristic of most of the pine family. This resinous scent, so strange to a grub that lives always in oak, ought to vex it, to trouble it; and it should show its displeasure by some kind of commotion, some attempt to get away. It did nothing of the kind: once it had found the right position in the groove it went to the end, as far as it could go, and made no further movement. Then I set before it, in its usual channel, a piece of camphor. Again no effect. Camphor was followed by naphthaline. Still no result. I do not think I am going too far when I deny the creature a sense of smell.

Taste is there no doubt. But such taste! The food is without variety: oak, for three years at a stretch, and nothing else. What can the grub's palate find to enjoy in this monotonous fare? The agreeable sensation of a fresh piece, oozing with sap; the uninteresting flavour of an over-dry piece. These, probably, are the only changes in the meal.

There remains the sense of touch, the universal passive sense common to all live flesh that quivers under the goad of pain. The Capricorn-grub, therefore, is limited to two senses, those of taste and touch, and both of these it possesses only in a very small degree. It is very little better off than Condillac's statue. The imaginary being created by the philosopher had one sense only, that of smell, equal in delicacy to our own; the real being, the oak-eater has two, which are inferior even when put together to the one sense of the statue. The latter plainly perceived the scent of a rose, and clearly distinguished it from any other.

A vain wish has often come to me in my dreams: to be able to think, for a few minutes, with the brain of my Dog, or to see the world with the eyes of a Gnat. How things would change in appearance! But they would change much more if understood only with the intellect of the grub. What has that incomplete creature learnt through its senses of touch and taste? Very little; almost nothing. It knows that the best bits of wood have a special kind of flavour, and that the sides of a passage, when not carefully smoothed, are painful to the skin. This is the limit of its wisdom. In comparison with this, the statue with the sensitive nostrils was a marvel of knowledge. It remembered, compared, judged, and reasoned. Can the Capricorn-grub remember? Can it reason? I described it a little time ago as a bit of intestine that crawls about. This description gives an answer to these questions. The grub has the sensations of a bit of intestine, no more and no less.

III

The Grub's Foresight

And this half-alive object, this *nothing-at-all*, is capable of marvellous foresight. It knows hardly anything of the present, but it sees very clearly into the future.

For three years on end the larva wanders about in the heart of the trunk. It goes up, goes down, turns to this side and that; it leaves one vein for another of better flavour, but without ever going too far from the inner depths, where the temperature is milder than near the surface, and greater safety reigns. But a day is at hand when the hermit must leave its safe retreat and face the perils of the outer world. Eating is not everything, after all; we have to get out of this.

But how? For the grub, before leaving the trunk, must turn into a long-horned Beetle. And though the grub, being well equipped with tools and muscular strength, finds no difficulty in boring through the wood and going where it pleases, it by no means follows that the coming Capricorn has the same powers. The Beetle's short spell of life must be spent in the open air. Will it be able to clear itself a way of escape?

It is quite plain, at all events, that the Capricorn will be absolutely unable to make use of the tunnel bored by the grub. This tunnel is a very long and very irregular maze, blocked with great heaps of wormed wood. It grows constantly smaller and smaller as it approaches the starting-point, because the larva entered the trunk as slim as a tiny bit of straw, whereas to-day it is as thick as one's finger. In its three years' wanderings it always dug its gallery to fit the size of its body. Evidently the road of the larva cannot be the Capricorn's way out. His overgrown antennæ, his long legs, his inflexible armour-plates would find the narrow, winding corridor impassable. The passage would have to be cleared of its wormed wood, and, moreover, greatly enlarged. It would be easier to attack the untouched timber and dig straight ahead. Is the insect capable of doing so? I determined to find out.

I made some cavities of suitable size in some oak logs that had been chopped in two, and in each of these cells I placed a Capricorn that had just been transformed from the grub. I then joined the two sides of the logs, fastening them together with wire. When June came I heard a sound of scraping inside the logs, and waited anxiously to see if the Capricorns would appear. They had hardly three-quarters of an inch to pierce. Yet not one came out. On opening the logs I found all my captives dead. A pinch of sawdust represented all they had done.

I had expected more from their sturdy mandibles. In spite of their boring-tools the hermits died for lack of skill. I tried enclosing some in reed-stumps, but even this comparatively easy work was too much for them. Some freed themselves, but others failed.

Notwithstanding his stalwart appearance the Capricorn cannot leave the tree-trunk by his own unaided efforts. The truth is that his way is prepared for him by the grub—that bit of intestine.

Some presentiment—to us an unfathomable mystery—causes the Capricorn-grub to leave its peaceful strong-hold in the very heart of the oak and wriggle towards the outside, where its foe the Woodpecker is quite likely to gobble it up. At the risk of its life it stubbornly digs and gnaws to the very bark. It leaves only the thinnest film, the slenderest screen, between itself and the world at large. Sometimes, even, the rash one opens the doorway wide.

This is the Capricorn's way out. The insect has but to file the screen a little with his mandibles, to bump against it with his forehead, in order to bring it down. He will even have nothing at all to do when the doorway is open, as often happens. The unskilled carpenter, burdened with his extravagant head-dress, will come out from the darkness through this opening when the summer heat arrives.

As soon as the grub has attended to the important business of making a doorway into the world, it begins to busy itself with its transformation into a Beetle. First, it requires space for the purpose. So it retreats some distance down its gallery, and in the side of the passage digs itself a transformation-chamber more sumptuously furnished and barricaded than any I have ever seen. It is a roomy hollow with curved walls, three to four inches in length and wider than it is high. The width of the cell gives the insect a certain degree of freedom of movement when the time comes for forcing the barricade, which is more than a close-fitting case would do.

The barricade—a door which the larva builds as a protection from danger—is twofold, and often threefold. Outside, it is a stack of woody refuse, of particles of chopped timber; inside, a mineral lid, a concave cover, all in one piece, of a chalky white. Pretty often, but not always, there is added to these two layers an inner casing of shavings.

Behind this threefold door the larva makes its arrangements for its transformation. The sides of the chamber are scraped, thus providing a sort of down formed of ravelled woody fibres, broken into tiny shreds. This velvety stuff is fixed on the wall, in a thick coating, as fast as it is made. The chamber is thus padded throughout with a fine swan's-down, a delicate precaution taken by the rough grub out of kindness for the tender creature it will become when it has cast its skin.

Let us now go back to the most curious part of the furnishing, the cover or inner door of the entrance. It is like an oval skull-cap, white and hard as chalk, smooth within and rough without, with some resemblance to an acorn-cup. The rough knots show that the material is supplied in small, pasty mouthfuls, which become solid outside in little lumps. The animal does not remove them, because it is unable to get at them; but the inside surface is polished, being within the grub's reach. This singular lid is as hard and brittle as a flake of limestone. It is, as a matter of fact, composed solely of carbonate of lime, and a sort of cement which gives consistency to the chalky paste.

I am convinced that this stony deposit comes from a particular part of the grub's stomach, called the chylific ventricle. The chalk is kept separate from the food, and is held in reserve until the right time comes to discharge it. This freestone factory causes me no astonishment. It serves for various chemical works in

different grubs when undergoing transformation. Certain Oil-
beetles keep refuse in it, and several kinds of Wasps use it to
manufacture the shellac with which they varnish the silk of their
cocoons.

When the exit way is prepared, and the cell upholstered in
velvet and closed with a threefold barricade, the industrious
grub has finished its task. It lays aside its tools, sheds its skin,
and becomes a pupa—weakness personified, in the swaddling-clothes of a cocoon. The head is always turned towards
the door. This is a trifling detail in appearance; but in reality it is everything. To lie this way or that in the long cell is a
matter of great indifference to the grub, which is very supple, turning easily in its narrow lodging and adopting whatever position it pleases. The coming Capricorn will not enjoy
the same privileges. Stiffly encased in his horny armour, he
will not be able to turn from end to end; he will not even be
capable of bending, if some sudden curve should make the
passage difficult. He must, without fail, find the door in
front of him, or he will perish in the transformation-room. If
the grub should forget this little matter, and lie down to
sleep with its head at the back of the cell, the Capricorn
would be infallibly lost. His cradle would become a hopeless
dungeon.

But there is no fear of this danger. The "bit of intestine"
knows too much about the future to neglect the formality of
keeping its head at the door. At the end of spring the Capricorn,
now in possession of his full strength, dreams of the joys of the
sun, of the festivals of light. He wants to get out.

What does he find before him? First, a heap of filings easily
dispersed with his claws; next, a stone lid which he need not
even break into fragments, for it comes undone in one piece. It
is removed from its frame with a few pushes of the forehead, a
few tugs of the claws. In fact, I find the lid intact on the threshold of the abandoned cell. Last comes a second mass of woody
remnants as easy to scatter as the first. The road is now free: the
Capricorn has but to follow the wide vestibule, which will lead
him, without any possibility of mistake, to the outer exit. Should
the doorway not be open, all that he has to do is to gnaw through

a thin screen, an easy task. Behold him outside, his long antennæ quivering with excitement.

What have we learnt from him? Nothing from him, but much
from his grub. This grub, so poor in organs of sensation, gives us
much to think about. It knows that the coming Beetle will not
be able to cut himself a road through the oak, and it therefore
opens one for him at its own risk and peril. It knows that the
Capricorn, in his stiff armour, will never be able to turn round
and make for the opening of the cell; and it takes care to fall into
its sleep of transformation with its head towards the door. It
knows how soft the pupa's flesh will be, and it upholsters the
bedroom with velvet. It knows that the enemy is likely to break
in during the slow work of the transformation, and so, to make
a protection against attack, it stores lime inside its stomach. It
knows the future with a clear vision, or, to be accurate, it
behaves as if it knew the future.

What makes it act in this way? It is certainly not taught by the
experiences of its senses. What does it know of the outside
world? I repeat—as much as a bit of intestine can know. And
this senseless creature astounds us! I regret that the philosopher
Condillac, instead of creating a statue that could smell a rose,
did not gift it with an instinct. How soon he would have seen
that the animals—including man—have powers quite apart
from the senses; inspirations that are born with them, and are
not the result of learning.

This curious life and this marvellous foresight are not confined to one kind of grub. Besides the Capricorn of the Oak
there is the Capricorn of the Cherry-tree. In appearance the latter is an exact copy of the former, on a much smaller scale; but
the little Capricorn has different tastes from its large kinsman's.
If we search the heart of the cherry-tree it does not show us a
single grub anywhere: the entire population lives between the
bark and the wood. This habit is only varied when transformation is at hand. Then the grub of the cherry-tree leaves the surface, and scoops out a cavity at a depth of about two inches.
Here the walls are bare: they are not lined with the velvety
fibres dear to the Capricorn of the Oak. The entrance is
blocked, however, by sawdust, and a chalky lid similar to the

other except in point of size. Need I add that the grub lies down and goes to sleep with his head against the door? Not one forgets to take this precaution.

There is also a Saperda of the Poplar and a Saperda of the Cherry-tree. They have the same organisation and the same tools; but the former follows the methods of the Capricorn of the Oak, while the latter imitates the Capricorn of the Cherry-tree.

The poplar-tree is also inhabited by the Bronze Buprestis, which takes no defensive measures before going to sleep. It makes no barricade, no heap of shavings. And in the apricot-tree the Nine-spotted Buprestis behaves in the same way. In this case the grub is inspired by its intuitions to alter its plan of work to suit the coming Beetle. The perfect insect is a cylinder; the grub is a strap, a ribbon. The former, which wears unyielding armour, needs a cylindrical passage; the latter needs a very low tunnel, with a roof that it can reach with the pads on its back. The grub therefore changes its manner of boring: yesterday the gallery, suited to a wandering life in the thickness of the wood, was a wide burrow with a very low ceiling, almost a slot; to-day the passage is cylindrical. A gimlet could not bore it more accurately. This sudden change in the system of roadmaking on behalf of the coming insect once more shows us the foresight of this "bit of intestine."

I could tell you of many other wood-eaters. Their tools are the same; yet each species displays special methods, tricks of the trade that have nothing to do with the tools. These grubs, then, like so many insects, show us that instinct is not made by the tools, so to speak, but that the same tools may be used in various ways.

To continue the subject would be monotonous. The general rule stands out very clearly from these facts: the wood-eating grubs prepare the path of deliverance for the perfect insect, which will merely have to pass a barricade of shavings or pierce a screen of bark. By a curious reversal of the usual state of things, infancy is here the season of energy, of strong tools, of stubborn work; mature age is the season of leisure, of industrial ignorance, of idle diversions, without trade or profession. The providence of the human infant is the mother; here the baby grub is the mother's providence. With its patient tooth, which neither the peril of the outside world nor the difficult task of boring through hard wood is able to discourage, it clears away for her to the supreme delights of the sun.

CHAPTER XV

Locusts

I

Their Value

"Mind you're ready, children, to-morrow morning before the sun gets too hot. We're going Locust-hunting."

This announcement throws the household into great excitement at bed-time. What do my little helpers see in their dreams? Blue wings, red wings, suddenly flung out like fans; long saw-toothed legs, pale blue or pink, which kick out when we hold their owners in our fingers; great shanks that act like springs, and make the insect leap forward as though shot from a catapult.

If there be one peaceful and safe form of hunting, one in which both old age and childhood can share, it is Locust-hunting. What delicious mornings we owe to it! How delightful, when the mulberries are ripe, to pick them from the bushes! What excursions we have had, on the slopes covered with thin, tough grass, burnt yellow by the sun! I have vivid memories of such mornings, and my children will have them too.

Little Paul has nimble legs, a ready hand, and a piercing eye. He inspects the clumps of everlastings, and peers closely into the bushes. Suddenly a big Grey Locust flies out like a little bird. The hunter first makes off at full speed, then stops and gazes in wonder at this mock Swallow flying far away. He will have better luck another time. We shall not go home without a few of those magnificent prizes.

Marie Pauline, who is younger than her brother, watches patiently for the Italian Locust, with his pink wings and carmine hind-legs; but she really prefers another, the most ornamented of them all. Her favourite wears a St. Andrew's cross on the small of his back, which is marked by four white, slanting stripes. He wears, too, patches of green, the colour of verdigris on bronze. With her hand raised in the air, ready to swoop down, she approaches very softly, stooping low. *Whoosh!* That's done it! The treasure is quickly thrust head-first into a paper funnel, and plunges with one bound to the bottom of it.

One by one our boxes are filled. Before the heat becomes too great to bear we are in possession of a number of specimens. Imprisoned in my cages, perhaps they will teach us something. In any case the Locusts have given pleasure to three people at a small cost.

Locusts have a bad reputation, I know. The textbooks describe them as noxious. I take the liberty of doubting whether they deserve this reproach, except, of course, in the case of the terrible ravagers who are the scourge of Africa and the East. Their ill repute has been fastened on all Locusts, though they are, I consider, more useful than harmful. As far as I know, our peasants have never complained of them. What damage do they do?

They nibble the tops of the tough grasses which the Sheep refuses to touch; they prefer the thin, poor grass to the fat pastures; they browse on barren land that can support none but them; they live on food that no stomach but theirs could use.

Besides, by the time they frequent the fields the green wheat—the only thing that might tempt them—has long ago yielded its grain and disappeared. If they happen to get into the kitchen-gardens and take a few bites, it is not a crime. A man can console himself for a piece bitten out of a leaf or two of salad.

To measure the importance of things by one's own turnip-patch is a horrible method. The short-sighted man would upset the order of the universe rather than sacrifice a dozen plums. If he thinks of the insect at all, it is only to kill it.

And yet, think what the consequences would be if all the Locusts were killed. In September and October the Turkeys are driven into the stubble, under charge of a child armed with two long reeds. The expanse over which the gobbling flock slowly spreads is bare, dry, and burnt by the sun. At the most, a few ragged thistles raise their heads. What do the birds do in this famine-stricken desert? They cram themselves, that they may do honour to the Christmas table; they wax fat; their flesh becomes firm and good to eat. And pray, what do they cram themselves with? With Locusts. They snap them up, one here one there, till their greedy crops are filled with the delicious stuffing, which costs nothing, though its rich flavour will greatly improve the Christmas Turkey.

When the Guinea-fowl roams about the farm, uttering her rasping cry, what is it she seeks? Seeds, no doubt; but above all Locusts, which puff her out under the wings with a pad of fat, and give a better flavour to her flesh. The Hen, too, much to our advantage, is just as fond of them. She well knows the virtues of that dainty dish, which acts as a tonic and makes her lay more eggs. When left at liberty she rarely fails to lead her family to the stubble-fields, so that they may learn to snap up the nice mouthful skilfully. In fact, every bird in the poultry-yard finds the Locust a valuable addition to his bill of fare.

It is still more important outside the poultry-yard. Any who is a sportsman, and knows the value of the Red-legged Partridge, the glory of our southern hills, should open the crop of the bird he has just shot. He will find it, nine times out of ten, more or less crammed with Locusts. The Partridge dotes on them, preferring them to seeds as long as he can catch them. This highly-flavoured, nourishing fare would almost make him forget the existence of seeds, if it were only there all the year round.

The Wheat-ear, too, who is so good to eat, prefers the Locust to any other food. And all the little birds of passage which, when autumn comes, call a halt in Provence before their great pilgrimage, fatten themselves with Locusts as a preparation for the journey.

Nor does man himself scorn them. An Arab author tells us:

"Grasshoppers"—(he means Locusts)—"are of good nourishment for men and Camels. Their claws, wings, and head are taken away, and they are eaten fresh or dried, either roast or boiled, and served with flesh, flour, and herbs.

". . . Camels eat them greedily, and are given them dried or roast, heaped in a hollow between two layers of charcoal. Thus also do the Nubians eat them. . . .

"Once, when the Caliph Omar was asked if it were lawful to eat Grasshoppers, he made answer:

"'Would that I had a basket of them to eat.'"

"Wherefore, from this testimony, it is very sure that, by the Grace of God, Grasshoppers were given to man for his nourishment."

Without going as far as the Arab I feel prepared to say that the Locust is a gift of God to a multitude of birds. Reptiles also hold him in esteem. I have found him in the stomach of the Eyed Lizard, and have often caught the little Grey Lizard of the walls in the act of carrying him off.

Even the fish revel in him, when good fortune brings him to them. The Locust leaps blindly, and without definite aim: he comes down wherever he is shot by the springs in his legs. If the place where he falls happens to be water, a fish gobbles him up at once. Anglers sometimes bait their hooks with a specially attractive Locust.

As for his being fit nourishment for man, except in the form of Partridge and young Turkey, I am a little doubtful. Omar, the mighty Caliph who destroyed the library of Alexandria, wished for a basket of Locusts, it is true, but his digestion was evidently better than his brains. Long before his day St. John the Baptist lived in the desert on Locusts and wild honey; but in his case they were not eaten because they were good.

Wild honey from the pots of the Mason-bees is very agreeable food, I know. Wishing to taste the Locust also I once caught some, and had them cooked as the Arab author advised. We all of us, big and little, tried the queer dish at dinner. It was much nicer than the Cicadæ praised by Aristotle. I would go to the length of saying it is good—without, however, feeling any desire for more.

II

Their Musical Talent

The Locust possesses musical powers wherewith to express his joys. Consider him at rest, blissfully digesting his meal and enjoying the sunshine. With sharp strokes of the bow, three or four times repeated with a pause between, he plays his tune. He scrapes his sides with his great hind-legs, using now one, now the other, and now both at a time.

The result is very poor, so slight indeed that I am obliged to make use of little Paul's sharp ear to make sure that there is a sound at all. Such as it is, it is like the squeaking of a needle-point pushed across a sheet of paper. There you have the whole song, which is very nearly silence.

We can expect no more than this from the Locust's very unfinished instrument. There is nothing here like the Cricket's toothed bow and sounding-board. The lower edge of the wing-cases is rubbed by the thighs, but though both wing-cases and thighs are powerful they have no roughnesses to supply friction, and there is no sign of teeth.

This artless attempt at a musical instrument can produce no more sound than a dry membrane will emit when you rub it yourself. And for the sake of this small result the insect lifts and lowers its thigh in sharp jerks, and appears perfectly satisfied. It rubs its sides very much as we rub our hands together in sign of contentment, with no intention of making a sound. That is its own particular way of expressing its joy in life.

Observe the Locust when the sky is partly covered with clouds, and the sun shines only at times. There comes a rift in the clouds. At once the thighs begin to scrape, becoming more and more active as the sun grows hotter. The strains are brief, but they are repeated as long as the sunshine continues. The sky becomes overcast. Then and there the song ceases; but is renewed with the next gleam of sunlight, always in brief out-burst. There is no mistaking it: here, in these fond lovers of the light, we have a mere expression of happiness. The Locust has his moments of gaiety when his crop is full and the sun is kind.

Not all the Locusts indulge in this joyous rubbing.

The Tryxalis, who has a pair of immensely long hind-legs, keeps up a gloomy silence when even the sunshine is brightest. I have never seen him move his shanks like a bow; he seems unable to use them—so long are they—for anything but hopping.

The big Grey Locust, who often visits me in the enclosure,

even in the depth of winter, is also dumb in consequence of the excessive length of his legs. But he has a peculiar way of diverting himself. In calm weather, when the sun is hot, I surprise him in the rosemary bushes with his wings unfurled and fluttering rapidly, as though for flight. He keeps up this performance for a quarter of an hour at a time. His fluttering is so gentle, in spite of its extreme speed, that it creates hardly any rustling sound.

Others are still worse off. One of these is the Pedestrian Locust, who strolls on foot on the ridges of the Ventoux amid sheets of Alpine flowers, silvery, white, and rosy. His colouring is as fresh as that of the flowers. The sunlight, which is clearer on those heights than it is below, has made him a costume combining beauty with simplicity. His body is pale brown above and yellow below, his big thighs are coral red, his hind-legs a glorious azure-blue, with an ivory anklet in front. But in spite of being such a dandy he wears too short a coat.

His wing-cases are merely wrinkled slips, and his wings no more than stumps. He is hardly covered as far as the waist. Any one seeing him for the first time takes him for a larva, but he is indeed the full-grown insect, and he will wear this incomplete garment to the end.

With this skimpy jacket of course, music is impossible to him. The big thighs are there; but there are no wing-cases, no grating edge for the bow to rub upon. The other Locusts cannot be described as noisy, but this one is absolutely dumb. In vain have the most delicate ears listened with all their might. This silent one must have other means of expressing his joys. What they are I do not know.

Nor do I know why the insect remains without wings, a plodding wayfarer, when his near kinsmen on the same Alpine slopes have excellent means of flying. He possesses the beginnings of wings and wing-cases, gifts inherited by the larva; but he does not develop these beginnings and make use of them. He persists in hopping, with no further ambition: he is satisfied to go on foot, to remain a Pedestrian Locust, when he might, one would think, acquire wings. To flit rapidly from crest to crest, over valleys deep in snow, to fly from one pasture to another, would certainly be great advantages to him. His fellow-dwellers on the mountain-tops possess wings and are all the better for them. It would be very profitable to extract from their sheaths the sails he keeps packed away in useless stumps; and he does not do it. Why?

No one knows why. Anatomy has these puzzles, these surprises, these sudden leaps, which defy our curiosity. In the presence of such profound problems the best thing is to bow in all humility, and pass on.

III

Their Early Days

The Locust mother is not, in all cases, a model of affection. The Italian Locust, having laboriously half-buried herself in the sand, lays her eggs there and immediately bounds away. She gives not a look at the eggs, nor makes the least attempt to cover the hole where they lie. It closes of its own accord, as best it can, by the natural falling-in of the sand. It is an extremely casual performance, marked by an utter absence of maternal care.

Others do not forsake their eggs so recklessly. The ordinary Locust with the blue-and-black wings, for instance, after leaving her eggs in the sand, lifts her hind-legs high, sweeps some sand into the hole, and presses it down by stamping it rapidly. It is a pretty sight to watch the swift action of her slender legs, giving alternate kicks to the opening they are plugging. With this lively trampling the entrance to the home is closed and hidden away. The hole that contains the eggs completely disappears, so that no ill-intentioned creature could find it by sight alone.

Nor is this all. The power that works the two rammers lies in the hinder thighs, which, as they rise and fall, scrape lightly against the edge of the wing-cases. This scraping produces a faint sound, similar to that with which the insect placidly lulls itself to sleep in the sun.

The Hen salutes with a song of gladness the egg she just laid; she announces her performance to the whole neighbourhood. The Locust celebrates the same event with her thin scraper. "I have buried underground," she says, "the treasure of the future."

Having made the nest safe she leaves the spot, refreshes herself after her exertions with a few mouthfuls of green stuff, and prepares to begin again.

The Grey Locust mother is armed at the tip of her body—and so are other female Locusts in varying degrees—with four short tools, arranged in pairs and shaped like a hooked fingernail. On the upper pair, which are larger than the others, these hooks are turned upwards; on the lower and smaller pair they are turned downwards. They form a sort of claw, and are scooped out slightly, like a spoon. These are the pick-axes, the boring-tools with which the Grey Locust works. With these she bites into the soil, lifting the dry earth a little, as quietly as if she were digging in soft mould. She might be working in butter; and yet what the bore digs into is hard, unyielding earth.

The best site for laying the eggs is not always found at the first attempt. I have seen the mother make five wells one after the other before finding a suitable place. When at last the business is over, and the insect begins to rise from the hole in which she is partly buried, one can see that she is covering her eggs with milk-white foam, similar to that of the Mantis.

This foamy matter often forms a button at the entrance to the well, a knot which stands up and attracts the eye by its whiteness against the grey background of the soil. It is soft and sticky, but hardens pretty soon. When this closing button is finished the mother moves away and troubles no more about her eggs, of which she lays a fresh batch elsewhere after a few days.

Sometimes the foamy paste does not reach the surface; it stops some way down, and before long is covered with the sand that slips from the edge. But in the case of my Locusts in captivity I always know, even when it is concealed, exactly where the barrel of eggs lies. Its structure is always the same, though there are variations in detail. It is always a sheath of solidified foam. Inside, there is nothing but foam and eggs. The eggs all lie in the lower portion, packed one on top of another; and the upper part consists only of soft, yielding foam. This portion plays an important part when the young larvæ are hatched. I will call it the ascending-shaft.

The wonderful egg-casket of the Mantis is not the result of

any special talent which the mother can exercise at will. It is due
to mechanism. It happens of itself. In the same way the Locusts
have no industry of their own, especially devised for laying eggs
in a keg of froth. The foam is produced with the eggs, and the
arrangement of eggs at the bottom and centre, and froth on the
outside and the top, is purely mechanical.

There are many Locusts whose egg-cases have to last through
the winter, since they do not open until the fine weather returns.
Though the soil is loose and dusty at first, it becomes caked
together by the winter rains. Supposing that the hatching takes
place a couple of inches below the surface, how is this crust, this
hard ceiling, to be broken? How is the larva to come up from
below? The mother's unconscious art has arranged for that.

The young Locust finds above him, when he comes out of the
egg, not rough sand and hardened earth, but a straight tunnel,
with solid walls that keep all difficulties away. This ascending-
shaft is full of foam, which the larva can easily penetrate, and
which will bring him quite close to the surface. Here only a finger's-breadth of serious work remains to be done.

The greater part of the journey, therefore, is accomplished
without effort. Though the Locust's building is done quite
mechanically, without the least intelligence, it is certainly singu-
larly well devised.

The little creature has now to complete his deliverance. On
leaving his shell he is of a whitish colour, clouded with light red.
His progress is made by worm-like movements; and, so that it
may be as easy as possible, he is hatched, like the young
Grasshopper, in a temporary jacket which keeps his antennæ
and legs closely fixed to his body. Like the White-faced Decticus
he keeps his boring-tool at his neck. Here there is a kind of
tumour that swells and subsides alternately, and strikes the
obstacle before it as regularly as a piston. When I see this soft
bladder trying to overcome the hardness of the earth I come to
the unhappy creature's aid, and damp the layer of soil.

Even then the work is terribly hard. How it must labour, the
poor little thing, how it must persevere with its throbbing head
and writhing loins, before it can clear a passage for itself! The
wee mite's efforts show us plainly that the journey to the light of

day is an enormous undertaking, in which the greater number would die but for the help of the exit-tunnel, the mother's work.

When the tiny insect reaches the surface at last, it rests for a moment to recover from all that fatigue. Then suddenly the blister swells and throbs, and the temporary jacket splits. The rags are pushed back by the hind-legs, which are the last to be stripped. The thing is done: the creature is free, pale in colouring as yet, but possessing its final form as a larva.

Immediately the hind-legs, hitherto stretched in a straight line, fall into the correct position. The legs fold under the great thighs, and the spring is ready to work. It works, Little Locust makes his entrance into the world, and hops for the first time. I offer him a bit of lettuce the size of my fingernail. He refuses it. Before taking nourishment he must first mature and grow in the sun.

IV

Their Final Change

I have just beheld a stirring sight: the last change of a Locust, the full-grown insect emerging from his larval skin. It is magnificent. The object of my enthusiasm is the Grey Locust, the giant who is so common on the vines at vintage-time, in September. On account of his size—he is as long as my finger—he is easier to observe than any other of his tribe. The event took place in one of my cages.

The fat, ungraceful larva, a rough sketch of the perfect insect, is usually pale green; but some are blue-green, dirty yellow, red-brown, or even ashen-grey, like the grey of the full-grown Locust. The hind-legs, which are as powerful as those of mature age, have a great haunch striped with red and a long shank shaped like a two-edged saw.

The wing-cases are at present two skimpy, triangular pinions, of which the free ends stand up like pointed gables. These two coat-tails, of which the material seems to have been clipped short with ridiculous meanness, just cover the creature's nakedness at the small of the back, and shelter two lean strips, the germs of the wings. In brief, the sumptuous slender sails of the near future are at present sheer rags, of such meagre size as to be grotesque. From these miserable envelopes there will come a marvel of stately elegance.

The first thing to be done is to burst the old tunic. All along the corselet of the insect there is a line that is weaker than the rest of the skin. Waves of blood can be seen throbbing within, rising and falling alternately, distending the skin until at last it splits at the line of least resistance, and opens as though the two symmetrical halves had been soldered. The split is continued some little way back, and runs between the fastenings of the wings: it goes up the head as far as the base of the antennæ, where it sends a short branch to right and left.

Through this break the back is seen, quite soft, pale, hardly tinged with grey. Slowly it swells into a larger and larger hunch. At last it is wholly released. The head follows, pulled out of its mask, which remains in its place, intact in the smallest particular, but looking strange with its great eyes that do not see. The sheaths of the antennæ, without a wrinkle, with nothing out of order, and with their usual position unchanged, hang over this dead face, which is now half transparent.

This means that the antennæ within, although fitted into narrow sheaths that enclose them as precisely as gloves, are able to withdraw without disturbing the covers in the smallest degree, or even wrinkling them. The contents manage to slip out as easily as a smooth, straight object could slip from a loose sheath. This mechanism is even more remarkable in the case of the hind-legs.

Now it is the turn of the fore-legs and intermediary legs to shed their armlets and gauntlets, always without the least rent, however small, without a crease of rumpled material, or a trace of any change in the natural position. The insect is now fixed to the top of the cage only by the claws of the long hind-legs. It hangs perpendicularly by four tiny hooks, head downwards, and it swings like a pendulum if I touch the wire-gauze.

The wing-cases and wings now emerge. These are four narrow strips, faintly grooved and looking like bits of paper ribbon. At this stage they are scarcely a quarter of their final length. They are so limp that they bend under their own weight and sprawl along the insect's sides in the wrong direction, with their points towards the head of the Locust. Imagine four blades of thick grass, bent and battered by a rain-storm, and you will have a fair picture of the pitiable bunch formed by the future wings.

The hind-legs are next released. The great thighs appear, tinted on their inner surface with pale pink, which will soon turn into a streak of bright crimson. They come out of the sheath quite easily, for the thick haunch makes way for the tapering knuckle.

The shank is a different matter. The shank of the full-grown insect bristles throughout its length with a double row of hard, pointed spikes. Moreover, the lower extremity ends in four large spurs. It is a genuine saw, but with two parallel sets of teeth.

Now this awkwardly shaped skin is enclosed in a sheath that is formed in exactly the same way. Each spur is fitted into a similar spur, each tooth into the hollow of a similar tooth. And the sheath is as close and as thin as a coat of varnish.

Nevertheless the saw-like skin slips out of its long narrow case without catching in it at any point whatever. If I had not seen this happen over and over again I could never have believed it. The saw does no injury to the dainty scabbard which a puff of my breath is enough to tear; the formidable rake slips through without leaving the least scratch behind it.

One would expect that, because of the spiked armour, the envelope of the leg would strip off in scales coming loose of themselves, or would be rubbed off like dead skin. But the reality exceeds all possible expectation. From the spurs and spikes of the infinitely thin envelope there are drawn spurs and spikes so strong that they can cut soft wood. This is done without violence, the discarded skin remains where it was, hanging by the claws to the top of the cage, uncreased and untorn. The magnifying-glass shows not a trace of rough usage.

If it were suggested that one should draw out a saw from some sort of gold-beater's skin sheath which had been exactly moulded on the steel, and that one should perform the operation without making the least tear, one would simply laugh. The thing would be impossible. Yet Nature makes light of such impossibilities; she can realise the absurd, in case of need.

The difficulty is overcome in this way. While the leg is being liberated it is not rigid, as it will presently be. It is soft and highly flexible. Where it is exposed to view I see it bending and curving: it is as supple as elastic cord. And farther on, where it is hidden, it is certainly still softer, it is almost fluid. The teeth of the saw are there, but have none of their future sharpness. The spikes lie backwards when the leg is about to be drawn back: as it emerges they stand up and become solid. A few minutes later the leg has attained the proper state of stiffness.

And now the fine tunic is wrinkled and rumpled, and pushed back along the body towards the tip. Except at this point the Locust is bare. After a rest of twenty minutes he makes a supreme effort; he raises himself as he hangs, and grabs hold of his cast skin. Then he climbs higher, and fixes himself to the wire of the cage with his four front feet. He loosens the empty husk with one last shake, and it falls to the ground. The Locust's transformation is conducted in much the same way as the Cicada's.

The insect is now standing erect, and therefore the flexible wings are in the right position. They are no longer curved backwards like the petals of a flower, they are no longer upside down; but they still look shabby and insignificant. All that we see is a few wrinkles, a few winding furrows, which tell us that the stumps are bundles of cunningly folded material, arranged so as to take up as little space as possible.

Very gradually they expand, so gradually that their unfolding cannot be seen even under the microscope. The process continues for three hours. Then the wings and wing-cases stand up on the Locust's back like a huge set of sails, sometimes colourless, sometimes pale-green, like the Cicada's wings at the beginning. One is amazed at their size when one thinks of the paltry bundles that represented them at first. How could so much stuff find room there?

The fairy tale tells us of a grain of hempseed that contained the under-linen of a princess. Here is a grain that is even more astonishing. The one in the story took years and years to sprout and multiply, till at last it yielded the hemp required for the trousseau: the Locust's tiny bundle supplies a sumptuous set of sails in three hours. They are formed of exquisitely fine gauze, a network of innumerable tiny bars.

In the wing of the larva we can see only a few uncertain outlines of the future lace-work. There is nothing to suggest the marvellous fabric whose every mesh will have its form and place arranged for it, with absolute exactness. Yet it is there, as the oak is inside the acorn.

There must be something to make the matter of the wing shape itself into a sheet of gauze, into a labyrinth of meshes. There must be an original plan, an ideal pattern which gives each atom its proper place. The stones of our buildings are arranged in accordance with the architect's plan; they form an imaginary building before they exist as a real one. In the same way a Locust's wing, that sumptuous piece of lace emerging from a miserable sheath, speaks to us of another Architect, the Author of the plans which Nature must follow in her labours.

CHAPTER XVI

The Anthrax Fly

I

A Strange Meal

I made the acquaintance of the Anthrax in 1855 at Carpentras, when I was searching the slopes of which I have already told you, the slopes beloved of the Anthophora-bees. Her curious pupa, so powerfully equipped to force an outlet for the perfect insect, which is incapable of the least effort, seemed worthy of investigation. For that pupa is armed with a plough-share in front, a trident at its tail, and rows of harpoons on its back, with which to rip open the Osmia-bee's cocoon and break through the hard crust of the hill-side.

Let us, some day in July, knock away the pebbles that fasten the nests of the Mason-bees to the sloping ground on which they are built. Loosened by the shock, the dome comes off cleanly, all in one piece. Moreover—and this is a great advantage—the cells are all exposed at the base of the nest, for at this point they have no other wall than the surface of the pebble. Without any scraping, which would be wearisome work for us and dangerous to the Bees, we have all the cells before our eyes, together with their contents—a silky, amber-yellow cocoon, as delicate and transparent as the skin of an onion. Let us split the dainty wrappers with the scissors, cell by cell, one after another. If fortune be at all kind, as it always is to the persevering, we shall end by finding cocoons harbouring two larvæ together, one more or less faded in appearance, the other fresh and plump. We shall also find some, no less plentiful, in which the withered larva is accompanied by a family of little grubs wriggling uneasily round it.

It is easy to see that a tragedy is happening under the cover of the cocoon. The flabby, faded larva is the Mason-bee's. A month ago, in June, having finished its ration of honey, it wove itself a silken sheath in which to take the long sleep that precedes its transformation. It was bulging with fat, and was a rich and a defenceless morsel for any enemy that could reach it. And enemies did reach it. In spite of obstacles that might well seem insurmountable, the wall of mortar and dome-shaped cover, the enemy grubs appeared in the secret retreat, and began to eat the sleeper. Three different species take part in this murderous work, often in the same nest, in adjoining cells. We will concern ourselves only with the Anthrax Fly.

The grub, when it has eaten its victim and is left alone in the Mason-bee's cocoon, is a naked worm, smooth, legless, and blind. It is creamy-white, and each of its segments or divisions forms a perfect ring, very much curved when at rest, but almost straight when disturbed. Including the head I can count thirteen segments, well-marked in the middle of the body, but in the fore-part difficult to distinguish. The white, soft head shows no sign of any mouth, and is no bigger than a tiny pin's head. The grub has four pale red stigmata, or openings through which to breathe, two in front and two behind, as is the rule among Flies. It has no walking-apparatus whatever; it is absolutely incapable of shifting its position. If I disturb its rest, it curves and straightens itself alternately, tossing about violently where it lies; but it does not manage to progress.

But the most interesting point about the grub of the Anthrax is its manner of eating. A most unexpected fact attracts our attention: the curious ease with which this larva leaves and returns to the Bee-grub on which it is feeding. After watching flesh-eating grubs at hundreds and hundreds of meals, I suddenly find myself confronted with a manner of eating that is entirely unlike anything I ever saw before.

This, for instance, is the Amophila-grub's way of devouring its caterpillar. A hole is made in the victim's side, and the head and neck of the grub dives deep into the wound. It never withdraws its head, never pauses to take breath. The voracious animal always goes forward, chewing, swallowing, digesting, until the caterpillar's skin is empty. Once the meal is begun, the creature does not budge as long as the food lasts. If moved by force it hesitates, and hunts about for the exact spot where it left off eating; for if the caterpillar be attacked at a fresh point it is liable to go bad.

In the case of the Anthrax-grub there is none of this mangling, none of this persistent clinging to the original wound. If I tease it with the tip of a pointed brush it at once retires, and there is no wound to be seen on the victim, no sign of broken skin. Soon the grub once more applies its pimple-head to its meal, at any point, no matter where, and keeps itself fixed there without any effort. If I repeat the touch with the brush I see the same sudden retreat and the same calm return to the meal.

The ease with which this larva grips, leaves, and regrips its victim, now here, now there, and always without a wound, shows that the mouth of the Anthrax is not armed with fangs that can dig into the skin and tear it. If the flesh were gashed by pincers of any kind, one or two attempts would be necessary before they could leave go or take hold again; and besides, the skin would be broken. There is nothing of the kind: the grub simply glues its mouth to its prey, and withdraws it. It does not chew its food like the other flesh-eating grub: it does not eat, it inhales.

This remarkable fact led me to examine the mouth under the microscope. It is a small conical crater, with yellowish-red sides and very faint lines running round it. At the bottom of this funnel is the opening of the throat. There is not the slightest trace of mandibles or jaws, or any object capable of seizing and grinding food. There is nothing at all but the bowl-shaped opening. I know of no other example of a mouth like this, which I can only compare to a cupping-glass. Its attack is a mere kiss, but what a cruel kiss!

To observe the working of this curious machine I placed a new-born Anthrax-grub, together with its prey, in a glass tube. Here I was able to watch the strange repast from beginning to end.

The Anthrax-grub—the Bee's uninvited guest—is fixed by its mouth or sucker to any convenient part of the plump Bee-grub. It is ready to break off its kiss suddenly, should anything disturb it, and to resume it as easily when it wishes. After three or four days of this curious contact the Bee-grub, formerly so fat, glossy, and healthy, begins to look withered. Her sides fall in, her fresh colour fades, her skin becomes covered with little folds, and she is evidently shrinking. A week is hardly passed when these signs of exhaustion increase to a startling degree. The victim is flabby and wrinkled, as though borne down by her own weight. If I move her from her place she flops and sprawls like a half-filled indiarubber bottle. But the kiss of the Anthrax goes on empty-ing her: soon she is but a sort of shrivelled bladder, growing smaller and smaller from hour to hour. At length, between the twelfth and fifteenth day, all that remains of the Mason-bee's larva is a little white grain, hardly as large as a pin's head.

If I soften this small remnant in water, and then blow into it through a very fine glass tube, the skin fills out and resumes the shape of the larva. There is no outlet anywhere for the com-pressed air. It is intact: it is nowhere broken. This proves that, under the cupping-glass of the Anthrax, the skin has been drained through its pores.

The devouring grub, in making its attack, chooses its moment very cunningly. It is but an atom. Its mother, a feeble Fly, has done nothing to help it. She has no weapons; and she is quite incapable of penetrating the Mason-bee's fortress. The future meal of the Anthrax has not been paralysed, nor injured in any way. The parasite arrives—we shall presently see how; it arrives, scarcely visible, and having made its preparations it installs itself upon its monstrous victim, whom it is going to drain to the very husk. And the victim, though not paralysed nor in any way lack-ing in vitality, lets it have its way, and is sucked dry without a tremor or a quiver of resistance. No corpse could show greater indifference to a bite.

Had the Anthrax-grub appeared upon the scene earlier, when the Bee-grub was eating her store of honey, things would sure-ly have gone badly with it. The victim, feeling herself bled to death by that ravenous kiss, would have protested with much wriggling of body and grinding of mandibles. The intruder would have perished. But at the hour chosen so wisely by it all danger is over. Enclosed in her silken sheath, the larva is in the torpid state that precedes her transformation into a Bee. Her condition is not death, but neither is it life. So there is no sign of irritation when I stir her with a needle, nor when the Anthrax-grub attacks her.

There is another marvellous point about the meal of the Anthrax-grub. The Bee-grub remains alive until the very end. Were she really dead it would, in less than twenty-four hours, turn a dirty-brown colour and decompose. But during the whole fortnight that the meal lasts, the butter-colour of the victim continues unaltered, and there is no sign of putrefaction. Life persists until the body is reduced to nothing. And yet, if I myself give her a wound, the whole body turns brown and soon begins to rot. The prick of a needle makes her decompose. A mere nothing kills it; the atrocious draining of its strength does not.

The only explanation I can suggest is this, and it is no more than a suggestion. Nothing but fluids can be drawn by the sucker of the Anthrax through the unpierced skin of the Bee-grub: no part of the breathing-apparatus or the nervous system can pass. As these two essentials remain uninjured, life goes on until the fluid contents of the skin are entirely exhausted. On the other hand, if I myself injure the larva of the Bee, I disturb the nervous or the air-conducting system, and the bruised part spreads a taint all over the body.

Liberty is a noble possession, even in an insignificant grub; but it has its dangers everywhere. The Anthrax escapes these dangers only on the condition of being, so to speak, muzzled. It finds its own way into the Bee's dwelling, quite independently of its mother. Unlike most of the other flesh-eating larvæ it is not fixed by its mother's care at the most suitable spot for its meal. It is perfectly free to attack its prey where it chooses. If it had a set of carving-tools, of jaws and mandibles, it would meet with a speedy death. It would split open its victim and bite it at random, and its food would rot. Its freedom of action would kill it.

II

The Way Out

There are other grub-eaters which drain their victims without wounding them, but not one, among those I know, reaches such perfection in this art as the Anthrax-grub. Nor can any be compared with the Anthrax as regards the means brought into play in order to leave the cell. The others, when they become perfect insects, have implements for mining and demolishing. They have stout mandibles, capable of digging the ground, of pulling down clay partition-walls, and even of grinding the Mason-bee's tough cement to powder. The Anthrax, in her final form, has nothing like this. Her mouth is a short, soft proboscis, good at most for soberly licking the sugary fluid from the flowers. Her slim legs are so feeble that to move a grain of sand would be too heavy a task for them, enough to strain every joint. Her great stiff wings, which must remain full-spread, do not allow her to slip through a narrow passage. Her delicate suit of downy velvet, from which you take the bloom by merely breathing on it, could not withstand the contact of rough tunnels. She is unable to enter the Mason-bee's cells to lay her egg, and equally unable to leave it when the time comes to free herself and appear in broad daylight.

And the grub, for its part, is powerless to prepare the way for the coming flight. That buttery little cylinder, owning no tools but a sucker so flimsy and small that it is barely visible through the magnifying-glass, is even weaker than the full-grown insect, which at least flies and walks. The Mason-bee's cell seems to this creature like a granite cave. How can it get out? The problems would be insoluble to these two incapables, if nothing else played its part.

Among insects the pupa—the transition stage, when the creature is no longer a grub but is not yet a perfect insect—is generally a striking picture of complete weakness. A sort of mummy, tightly bound in swaddling-clothes, motionless and unconscious, it awaits its transformation. Its tender flesh is hardly solid; its limbs are transparent as crystals, and are held fixed in their place, lest a movement should disturb the work of development. In the same way, to secure his recovery, a patient whose bones are broken is held bound in the surgeon's bandages.

Well, here, by a strange reversal of the usual state of things, a stupendous task is laid upon the pupa of the Anthrax. It is the pupa that has to toil, to strive, to exhaust itself in efforts to burst the wall and open the way out. To the pupa falls the desperate duty, to the full-grown insect the joy of resting in the sun. The result of these unusual conditions is that the pupa possesses a strange and complicated set of tools that is in no way suggested by the grub nor recalled by the perfect Fly. This set of tools includes a collection of ploughshares, gimlets, hooks, spears, and other implements that are not found in our trades nor named in our dictionaries. I will do my best to describe the strange gear.

By the time that July is nearly over the Anthrax has finished eating the Bee-grub. From that time until the following May it lies motionless in the Mason-bee's cocoon, beside the remains of its victim. When the fine days of May arrive it shrivels, and casts its skin; and it is then that the pupa appears, fully clad in a stout, reddish, horny hide.

The head is round and large, and is crowned on top and in front with a sort of diadem of six hard, sharp, black spikes, arranged in semi-circle. This sixfold plough-share is the chief digging-implement. Lower down the instrument is finished off with a separate group of two small black spikes, placed close together.

Four segments in the middle of the body are armed on the back with a belt of little horny arches, set in the skin upside down. They are arranged parallel to one another, and are finished at both ends with a hard, black point. The belt forms a double row of little thorns, with a hollow in between. There are about two hundred spikes on the four segments. The use of this rasp, or grater, is obvious: it helps the pupa to steady itself on the wall of the gallery as the work proceeds. Thus anchored on a host of points the brave pioneer is able to hit the obstacle harder with its crown of awls. Moreover, to make it more difficult for the instrument to recoil, there are long, stiff bristles, pointing backwards, scattered here and there among the rows of spikes. There are some also on other segments, and on the sides they are arranged in clusters. Two more belts of thorns, less powerful than the others, and a sheaf of eight spikes at the tip of the body—two of which are longer than the rest—completes the strange boring-machine that prepares an outlet for the feeble Anthrax.

About the end of May the colouring of the pupa alters, and shows that the transformation is close at hand. The head and fore-part of the creature become a handsome, shiny black, prophetic of the black livery worn by the coming insect. I was anxious to see the boring-tools in action, and, since this could not be done in natural conditions, I confined the Anthrax in a glass tube, between two thick stoppers of sorghum-pith. The space between the stoppers was about the same size as the Bee's cell, and the partitions, though not so strong as the Bee's masonry, were firm enough to withstand considerable effort. On the other hand the side-walls, being of glass, could not be gripped by the toothed belts, which made matters much harder for the worker.

No matter: in the space of a single day the pupa pierced the front partition, three-quarters of an inch thick. I saw it fixing its double ploughshare against the back partition, arching itself into a box, and then suddenly releasing itself and striking the stopper in front of it with its barbed forehead. Under the blows of the spikes the pith slowly crumbled to pieces, atom by atom. At long intervals the method of work changed. The animal drove its crown of awls into the pith, and fidgeted and swayed about for a time; then the blows began again. Now and then there were intervals of rest. At last the hole was made. The pupa slipped into it, but did not pass through entirely. The head and chest appeared beyond the hole, but the rest of the body remained held in the tunnel.

The glass cell certainly puzzled my Anthrax. The hole through the pith was wide and irregular: it was a clumsy breach and not a gallery. When made through the Mason-bee's walls it is fairly neat, and exactly of the animal's diameter. For narrowness and evenness in the exit-tunnel are necessary. The pupa always remains half-caught in it, and even pretty securely fixed by the graters on its back. Only the head and chest emerge into the outer air. A fixed support is indispensable, for without it the Anthrax could not issue from her horny sheath, unfurling her great wings and drawing out her slender legs.

She therefore remains steadily fixed by the graters on her back, in the narrow exit-gallery. All is now ready. The transfor-

mation begins. Two slits appear on the head: one along the forehead, and a second, crossing it, dividing the skull in two and
extending down the chest. Through this cross-shaped opening
the Anthrax Fly suddenly appears. She steadies herself upon her
trembling legs, dries her wings and takes to flight, leaving her
cast skin at the doorway of the gallery. The sad-coloured Fly has
five or six weeks before her wherein to explore the clay nests
amid the thyme and to take her small share of the joys of life.

III

The Way In

If you have paid attention to this story of the Anthrax Fly, you
must have noticed that it is incomplete. The Fox in the fable saw
how the Lion's visitors entered his den, but did not see how they
went out. With us the case is reversed: we know the way out of
the Mason-bee's fortress, but we do not know the way in. To
leave the cell whose owner it has eaten, the Anthrax becomes a
boring-tool. When the exit-tunnel is opened this tool splits like
a pod bursting in the sun, and from the strong framework there
escapes a dainty Fly. A soft bit of fluff that contrasts strangely
with the roughness of the prison whence it comes. On this point
we know pretty well what there is to know. But the entrance of
the grub into the cell puzzled me for a quarter of a century.

It is plain that the mother cannot place her egg in the Bee's
cell, which is closed and barricaded with a cement wall. To
pierce it she would have to become a boring-tool once more,
and get into the cast-off rags which she left at the doorway of the
exit-tunnel. She would have to become a pupa again. For the
full-grown Fly has no claws, nor mandibles, nor any implement
capable of working its way through the wall.

Can it be, then, the grub that makes its own way into the
storeroom, that same grub that we have seen sucking the life out
of the Bee's larva? Let us call the creature to mind: a little oily
sausage, which stretches and curls up just where it lies, without
being able to shift its position. Its body is a smooth cylinder, its
mouth a circular lip. It has no means whatever of moving; not
even a hair or a wrinkle to enable it to crawl. It can do nothing

but digest its food. It is even less able than the mother to make
its way into the Mason-bee's dwelling. And yet its provisions are
there: they must be reached: it is a matter of life and death. How
does the Fly set about it? In the face of this puzzle I resolved to
attempt an almost impossible task and watch the Anthrax from
the moment it left the egg.

Since these Flies are not really plentiful in my own neighbourhood I made an expedition to Carpentras, the dear little
town where I spent my twentieth year. The old college where I
made my first attempts as a teacher was unchanged in appearance. It still looked like a penitentiary. In my early days it was
considered unwholesome for boys to be gay and active, so our
system of education applied the remedy of melancholy and
gloom. Our houses of instruction were above all houses of cor-
rection. In a yard between four walls, a sort of bear-pit, the boys
fought to make room for their games under a spreading plane-
tree. All round it were cells like horseboxes, without light or air:
those were the class-rooms.

I saw, too, the shop where I used to buy tobacco as I came out
of the college; and also my former dwelling, now occupied by
monks. There, in the embrasure of a window, sheltered from
profane hands, between the closed outer shutters and the panes,
I kept my chemicals—bought for a few *sous* saved out of the
housekeeping money. My experiments, harmless or dangerous,
were made on a corner of the fire, beside the simmering broth.
How I should love to see that room again, where I pored over
mathematical problems; and my familiar friend the blackboard,
which I hired for five francs a year, and could never buy outright
for want of the necessary cash!

But I must return to my insects. My visit to Carpentras,
unfortunately, was made too late in the year to be very profitable. I saw only a few Anthrax Flies hovering round the face of
the cliff. Yet I did not despair, because it was plain that these few
were not there to take exercise, but to settle their families.

So I took my stand at the foot of the rock, under a broiling
sun, and for half a day I followed the movements of my Flies.
They flitted quietly in front of the slope, a few inches away from
the earthly covering. They went from one Bee's nest to another,

but without attempting to enter. For that matter, the attempt would be useless, for the galleries are too narrow to admit their spreading wings. So they simply explore the cliff, going to and fro, and up and down, with a flight that was now sudden, now smooth and slow. From time to time I saw one of them approach the wall and touch the earth suddenly with the tip of her body. The proceeding took no longer than the twinkling of an eye. When it was over the insect rested a moment, and then resumed flight.

I was certain that, at the moment when the Fly tapped the earth, she laid her eggs on the spot. Yet, though I rushed forward and examined the place with my lens, I could see no egg. In spite of the closest attention I could distinguish nothing. The truth is that my state of exhaustion, together with the blinding light and scorching heat, made it difficult for me to see anything. Afterwards, when I made the acquaintance of the tiny thing that comes out of that egg, my failure no longer surprised me: for even in the leisure and peace of my study I have the greatest difficulty in finding the infinitesimal creature. How then could I see the egg, worn out as I was under the sun-baked cliff?

None the less I was convinced that I had seen the Anthrax Flies strewing their eggs, one by one, on the spots frequented by the Bees who suit their grubs. They take no precaution to place the egg under cover, and indeed the structure of the mother makes any such precaution impossible. The egg, that delicate object, is laid roughly in the blazing sun, among grains of sand, in some wrinkle of the chalk. It is the business of the young grub to manage as best it can.

The next year I continued my investigations, this time on the Anthrax of the Chalicodoma, a Bee that abounds in my own neighbourhood. Every morning I took the field at nine o'clock, when the sun begins to be unendurable. I was prepared to come back with my head aching from the glare, if only I could bring home the solution of my puzzle. The greater the heat, the better my chances of success. What gives me torture fills the insect with delight; what prostrates me braces the Fly.

The road shimmers like a sheet of molten steel. From the

dusty, melancholy olive-trees rises a mighty, throbbing hum, the concert of the Cicadæ, who sway and rustle with increasing frenzy as the temperature increases. The Cicada of the Ash adds its strident scrapings to the single note of the Common Cicada. This is the moment! For five or six weeks, oftenest in the morning, sometimes in the afternoon, I set myself to explore the rocky waste.

There were plenty of the nests I wanted, but I could not see a single Anthrax on their surface. Not one settled in front of me to lay her egg. At most, from time to time, I could see one passing far away, with an impetuous rush. I would lose her in the distance; and that was all. It was impossible to be present at the laying of the egg. In vain I enlisted the services of the small boys who keep the sheep in our meadows, and talked to them of a big black Fly and the nests on which she ought to settle. By the end of August my last illusions were dispelled. Not one of us had succeeded in seeing the big black Fly perching on the dome of the Mason-bee.

The reason is, I believe, that she never perches there. She comes and goes in every direction across the stony plain. Her practised eye can detect, as she flies, the earthen dome which she is seeking, and having found it she swoops down, leaves her egg on it, and makes off without setting foot on the ground. Should she take a rest it will be elsewhere, on the soil, on a stone, on a tuft of lavender or thyme. It is no wonder that neither I nor my young shepherds could find her egg.

Meanwhile I searched the Mason-bees' nests for grubs just out of the egg. My shepherds procured me heaps of the nests, enough to fill baskets and baskets; and these I inspected at leisure on my work-table. I took the cocoons from the cells, and examined them within and without: my lens explored their innermost recesses, the sleeping larva, and the walls. Nothing, nothing, nothing! For a fortnight and more nests were searched and rejected, and heaped up in a corner. My study was crammed with them. In vain I ripped up the cocoons; I found nothing. It needed the sturdiest faith to make me persevere.

At last I saw, or seemed to see, something move on the Bee's larva. Was it an illusion? Was it a bit of down stirred by my breath? It was not an illusion; it was not a bit of down; it was really and truly a grub! But at first I thought the discovery unimportant, because I was so greatly puzzled by the little creature's appearance.

In a couple of days I was the owner of ten such worms and had placed each of them in a glass tube, together with the Bee-grub on which it wriggled. It was so tiny that the least fold of skin concealed it from my sight. After watching it one day through the lens I sometimes failed to find it again on the morrow. I would think it was lost: then it would move, and become visible once more.

For some time the belief had been growing in me that the Anthrax had *two* larval forms, a first and a second, the second being the form I knew, the grub we have already seen at its meals. Was this new discovery, I asked myself, the first form? Time showed me that it was. For at last I saw my little worms transform themselves into the grub I have already described, and make their first start at draining their victims with kisses. A few moments of satisfaction like those I then enjoyed make up for many a weary hour.

This tiny worm, the first form or "primary larva" of the Anthrax, is very active. It tramps over the fat sides of its victim, walking all round it. It covers the ground pretty quickly, buckling and unbuckling by turns, very much after the manner of the Looper-caterpillar. Its two ends are its chief points of support. When walking it swells out, and then looks like a bit of knotted string. It has thirteen rings or segments, including its tiny head, which bristles in front with short, stiff hairs. There are four other pairs of bristles on the lower surface, and with the help of these it walks.

For a fortnight the feeble grub remains in this condition, without growing, and apparently without eating. Indeed, what could it eat? In the cocoon there is nothing but the larva of the Mason-bee, and the worm cannot eat this before it has the sucker or mouth that comes with the second form. Nevertheless, as I said before, though it does not eat it is far from idle. It explores its future dish, and runs all over the neighborhood.

Now, there is a very good reason for this long fast. In the natural state of the Anthrax-grub it is necessary. The egg is laid by the mother on the surface of the nest, at a distance from the Bee's larva, which is protected by a thick rampart. It is the business of the new-born grub to make its way to its provisions, not by violence, of which it is incapable, but by patiently slipping through a maze of cracks. It is a very difficult task, even for this slender worm, for the Bee's masonry is exceedingly compact. There are no chinks due to bad building, no cracks due to the weather. I see but one weak point, and that only in a few nests: it is the line where the dome joins the surface of the stone. This weakness so seldom occurs that I believe the Anthrax-grub is able to find an entrance at any spot on the dome of the Bee's nest.

The grub is extremely weak, and has nothing but invincible patience. How long it takes to work its way through the masonry I cannot say. The work is so laborious and the worker so feeble! In some cases I believe it may be months before the slow journey is accomplished. So it is very fortunate, you see, that this first form of the Anthrax, which exists only in order to pierce the walls of the Bees' nest, should be able to live without food.

At last I saw my young worms shrink, and rid themselves of their outer skin. They then appeared as the grub I knew and was so anxiously expecting, the grub of the Anthrax, the cream-colored cylinder with the little button of a head. Fastening its round sucker to the Bee-grub, it began its meal. You know the rest.

Before taking leave of this tiny animal let us dwell for a moment on its marvellous instinct. Picture it as having just left the egg, just awakened to life under the fierce rays of the sun. The bare stone is its cradle; there is no one to welcome it as it enters the world, a mere thread of half-solid substance. Instantly it starts on its struggle with the flint. Obstinately it sounds each pore of the stone; it slips in, crawls on, retreats, begins again. What inspiration urges it towards its food, what compass guides it? What does it know of those depths, or of what lies in them? Nothing. What does the root of a plant know of the earth's fruitfulness? Again, nothing. Yet both the root and the worm make for the nourishing spot, Why? I do not understand. I do not even try to understand. The question is far above us.

We have now followed the complete history of the Anthrax. Its life is divided into four periods, each of which has its special form and its special work. The primary larva enters the Bees' nest, which contains provisions; the secondary larva eats those provisions; the pupa brings the insect to light by boring through the enclosing wall; the perfect insect strews its eggs. Then the story starts afresh.

A CATALOG OF SELECTED
DOVER BOOKS
IN ALL FIELDS OF INTEREST

A CATALOG OF SELECTED DOVER
BOOKS IN ALL FIELDS OF INTEREST

CONCERNING THE SPIRITUAL IN ART, Wassily Kandinsky. Pioneering work by father of abstract art. Thoughts on color theory, nature of art. Analysis of earlier masters. 12 illustrations. 80pp. of text. 5⅜ x 8½. 23411-8 Pa. $3.95

ANIMALS: 1,419 Copyright-Free Illustrations of Mammals, Birds, Fish, Insects, etc., Jim Harter (ed.). Clear wood engravings present, in extremely lifelike poses, over 1,000 species of animals. One of the most extensive pictorial sourcebooks of its kind. Captions. Index. 284pp. 9 x 12. 23766-4 Pa. $12.95

CELTIC ART: The Methods of Construction, George Bain. Simple geometric techniques for making Celtic interlacements, spirals, Kells-type initials, animals, humans, etc. Over 500 illustrations. 160pp. 9 x 12. (USO) 22923-8 Pa. $9.95

AN ATLAS OF ANATOMY FOR ARTISTS, Fritz Schider. Most thorough reference work on art anatomy in the world. Hundreds of illustrations, including selections from works by Vesalius, Leonardo, Goya, Ingres, Michelangelo, others. 593 illustrations. 192pp. 7⅛ x 10¼. 20241-0 Pa. $9.95

CELTIC HAND STROKE-BY-STROKE (Irish Half-Uncial from "The Book of Kells"): An Arthur Baker Calligraphy Manual, Arthur Baker. Complete guide to creating each letter of the alphabet in distinctive Celtic manner. Covers hand position, strokes, pens, inks, paper, more. Illustrated. 48pp. 8¼ x 11. 24336-2 Pa. $3.95

EASY ORIGAMI, John Montroll. Charming collection of 32 projects (hat, cup, pelican, piano, swan, many more) specially designed for the novice origami hobbyist. Clearly illustrated easy-to-follow instructions insure that even beginning papercrafters will achieve successful results. 48pp. 8¼ x 11. 27298-2 Pa. $3.50

THE COMPLETE BOOK OF BIRDHOUSE CONSTRUCTION FOR WOODWORKERS, Scott D. Campbell. Detailed instructions, illustrations, tables. Also data on bird habitat and instinct patterns. Bibliography. 3 tables. 63 illustrations in 15 figures. 48pp. 5¼ x 8½. 24407-5 Pa. $2.50

BLOOMINGDALE'S ILLUSTRATED 1886 CATALOG: Fashions, Dry Goods and Housewares, Bloomingdale Brothers. Famed merchants' extremely rare catalog depicting about 1,700 products: clothing, housewares, firearms, dry goods, jewelry, more. Invaluable for dating, identifying vintage items. Also, copyright-free graphics for artists, designers. Co-published with Henry Ford Museum & Greenfield Village. 160pp. 8¼ x 11. 25780-0 Pa. $10.95

HISTORIC COSTUME IN PICTURES, Braun & Schneider. Over 1,450 costumed figures in clearly detailed engravings–from dawn of civilization to end of 19th century. Captions. Many folk costumes. 256pp. 8⅜ x 11¾. 23150-X Pa. $12.95

STICKLEY CRAFTSMAN FURNITURE CATALOGS, Gustav Stickley and L. & J. G. Stickley. Beautiful, functional furniture in two authentic catalogs from 1910. 594 illustrations, including 277 photos, show settles, rockers, armchairs, reclining chairs, bookcases, desks, tables. 183pp. 6½ x 9¼.   23838-5 Pa. $9.95

AMERICAN LOCOMOTIVES IN HISTORIC PHOTOGRAPHS: 1858 to 1949, Ron Ziel (ed.). A rare collection of 126 meticulously detailed official photographs, called "builder portraits," of American locomotives that majestically chronicle the rise of steam locomotive power in America. Introduction. Detailed captions. xi + 129pp. 9 x 12.   27393-8 Pa. $12.95

AMERICA'S LIGHTHOUSES: An Illustrated History, Francis Ross Holland, Jr. Delightfully written, profusely illustrated fact-filled survey of over 200 American lighthouses since 1716. History, anecdotes, technological advances, more. 240pp. 8 x 10¾.
25576-X Pa. $12.95

TOWARDS A NEW ARCHITECTURE, Le Corbusier. Pioneering manifesto by founder of "International School." Technical and aesthetic theories, views of industry, economics, relation of form to function, "mass-production split" and much more. Profusely illustrated. 320pp. 6⅛ x 9¼. (USO)   25023-7 Pa. $9.95

HOW THE OTHER HALF LIVES, Jacob Riis. Famous journalistic record, exposing poverty and degradation of New York slums around 1900, by major social reformer. 100 striking and influential photographs. 233pp. 10 x 7⅞.
22012-5 Pa. $10.95

FRUIT KEY AND TWIG KEY TO TREES AND SHRUBS, William M. Harlow. One of the handiest and most widely used identification aids. Fruit key covers 120 deciduous and evergreen species; twig key 160 deciduous species. Easily used. Over 300 photographs. 126pp. 5⅜ x 8½.   20511-8 Pa. $3.95

COMMON BIRD SONGS, Dr. Donald J. Borror. Songs of 60 most common U.S. birds: robins, sparrows, cardinals, bluejays, finches, more—arranged in order of increasing complexity. Up to 9 variations of songs of each species.
Cassette and manual 99911-4 $8.95

ORCHIDS AS HOUSE PLANTS, Rebecca Tyson Northen. Grow cattleyas and many other kinds of orchids—in a window, in a case, or under artificial light. 63 illustrations. 148pp. 5⅜ x 8½.   23261-1 Pa. $4.95

MONSTER MAZES, Dave Phillips. Masterful mazes at four levels of difficulty. Avoid deadly perils and evil creatures to find magical treasures. Solutions for all 32 exciting illustrated puzzles. 48pp. 8¼ x 11.   26005-4 Pa. $2.95

MOZART'S DON GIOVANNI (DOVER OPERA LIBRETTO SERIES), Wolfgang Amadeus Mozart. Introduced and translated by Ellen H. Bleiler. Standard Italian libretto, with complete English translation. Convenient and thoroughly portable—an ideal companion for reading along with a recording or the performance itself. Introduction. List of characters. Plot summary. 121pp. 5¼ x 8½.
24944-1 Pa. $2.95

TECHNICAL MANUAL AND DICTIONARY OF CLASSICAL BALLET, Gail Grant. Defines, explains, comments on steps, movements, poses and concepts. 15-page pictorial section. Basic book for student, viewer. 127pp. 5⅜ x 8½.
21843-0 Pa. $4.95

BRASS INSTRUMENTS: Their History and Development, Anthony Baines. Authoritative, updated survey of the evolution of trumpets, trombones, bugles, cornets, French horns, tubas and other brass wind instruments. Over 140 illustrations and 48 music examples. Corrected and updated by author. New preface. Bibliography. 320pp. 5⅜ x 8½. 27574-4 Pa. $9.95

HOLLYWOOD GLAMOR PORTRAITS, John Kobal (ed.). 145 photos from 1926-49. Harlow, Gable, Bogart, Bacall; 94 stars in all. Full background on photographers, technical aspects. 160pp. 8⅜ x 11¼. 23352-9 Pa. $12.95

MAX AND MORITZ, Wilhelm Busch. Great humor classic in both German and English. Also 10 other works: "Cat and Mouse," "Plisch and Plumm," etc. 216pp. 5⅜ x 8½. 20181-3 Pa. $6.95

THE RAVEN AND OTHER FAVORITE POEMS, Edgar Allan Poe. Over 40 of the author's most memorable poems: "The Bells," "Ulalume," "Israfel," "To Helen," "The Conqueror Worm," "Eldorado," "Annabel Lee," many more. Alphabetic lists of titles and first lines. 64pp. 5³⁄₁₆ x 8¼. 26685-0 Pa. $1.00

PERSONAL MEMOIRS OF U. S. GRANT, Ulysses Simpson Grant. Intelligent, deeply moving firsthand account of Civil War campaigns, considered by many the finest military memoirs ever written. Includes letters, historic photographs, maps and more. 528pp. 6⅛ x 9¼. 28587-1 Pa. $11.95

AMULETS AND SUPERSTITIONS, E. A. Wallis Budge. Comprehensive discourse on origin, powers of amulets in many ancient cultures: Arab, Persian Babylonian, Assyrian, Egyptian, Gnostic, Hebrew, Phoenician, Syriac, etc. Covers cross, swastika, crucifix, seals, rings, stones, etc. 584pp. 5⅜ x 8½. 23573-4 Pa. $12.95

RUSSIAN STORIES/PYCCKNE PACCKA3bl: A Dual-Language Book, edited by Gleb Struve. Twelve tales by such masters as Chekhov, Tolstoy, Dostoevsky, Pushkin, others. Excellent word-for-word English translations on facing pages, plus teaching and study aids, Russian/English vocabulary, biographical/critical introductions, more. 416pp. 5⅜ x 8½. 26244-8 Pa. $8.95

PHILADELPHIA THEN AND NOW: 60 Sites Photographed in the Past and Present, Kenneth Finkel and Susan Oyama. Rare photographs of City Hall, Logan Square, Independence Hall, Betsy Ross House, other landmarks juxtaposed with contemporary views. Captures changing face of historic city. Introduction. Captions. 128pp. 8¼ x 11. 25790-8 Pa. $9.95

AIA ARCHITECTURAL GUIDE TO NASSAU AND SUFFOLK COUNTIES, LONG ISLAND, The American Institute of Architects, Long Island Chapter, and the Society for the Preservation of Long Island Antiquities. Comprehensive, well-researched and generously illustrated volume brings to life over three centuries of Long Island's great architectural heritage. More than 240 photographs with authoritative, extensively detailed captions. 176pp. 8¼ x 11. 26946-9 Pa. $14.95

NORTH AMERICAN INDIAN LIFE: Customs and Traditions of 23 Tribes, Elsie Clews Parsons (ed.). 27 fictionalized essays by noted anthropologists examine religion, customs, government, additional facets of life among the Winnebago, Crow, Zuni, Eskimo, other tribes. 480pp. 6⅛ x 9¼. 27377-6 Pa. $10.95

FRANK LLOYD WRIGHT'S HOLLYHOCK HOUSE, Donald Hoffmann. Lavishly illustrated, carefully documented study of one of Wright's most controversial residential designs. Over 120 photographs, floor plans, elevations, etc. Detailed perceptive text by noted Wright scholar. Index. 128pp. 9¼ x 10¾. 27133-1 Pa. $11.95

THE MALE AND FEMALE FIGURE IN MOTION: 60 Classic Photographic Sequences, Eadweard Muybridge. 60 true-action photographs of men and women walking, running, climbing, bending, turning, etc., reproduced from rare 19th-century masterpiece. vi + 121pp. 9 x 12. 24745-7 Pa. $10.95

1001 QUESTIONS ANSWERED ABOUT THE SEASHORE, N. J. Berrill and Jacquelyn Berrill. Queries answered about dolphins, sea snails, sponges, starfish, fishes, shore birds, many others. Covers appearance, breeding, growth, feeding, much more. 305pp. 5¼ x 8¼. 23366-9 Pa. $8.95

GUIDE TO OWL WATCHING IN NORTH AMERICA, Donald S. Heintzelman. Superb guide offers complete data and descriptions of 19 species: barn owl, screech owl, snowy owl, many more. Expert coverage of owl-watching equipment, conservation, migrations and invasions, etc. Guide to observing sites. 84 illustrations. xiii + 193pp. 5⅜ x 8½. 27344-X Pa. $8.95

MEDICINAL AND OTHER USES OF NORTH AMERICAN PLANTS: A Historical Survey with Special Reference to the Eastern Indian Tribes, Charlotte Erichsen-Brown. Chronological historical citations document 500 years of usage of plants, trees, shrubs native to eastern Canada, northeastern U.S. Also complete identifying information. 343 illustrations. 544pp. 6½ x 9¼. 25951-X Pa. $12.95

STORYBOOK MAZES, Dave Phillips. 23 stories and mazes on two-page spreads: Wizard of Oz, Treasure Island, Robin Hood, etc. Solutions. 64pp. 8¼ x 11. 23628-5 Pa. $2.95

NEGRO FOLK MUSIC, U.S.A., Harold Courlander. Noted folklorist's scholarly yet readable analysis of rich and varied musical tradition. Includes authentic versions of over 40 folk songs. Valuable bibliography and discography. xi + 324pp. 5⅜ x 8½. 27350-4 Pa. $9.95

MOVIE-STAR PORTRAITS OF THE FORTIES, John Kobal (ed.). 163 glamor, studio photos of 106 stars of the 1940s: Rita Hayworth, Ava Gardner, Marlon Brando, Clark Gable, many more. 176pp. 8⅝ x 11¼. 23546-7 Pa. $12.95

BENCHLEY LOST AND FOUND, Robert Benchley. Finest humor from early 30s, about pet peeves, child psychologists, post office and others. Mostly unavailable elsewhere. 73 illustrations by Peter Arno and others. 183pp. 5⅜ x 8½. 22410-4 Pa. $6.95

YEKL and THE IMPORTED BRIDEGROOM AND OTHER STORIES OF YIDDISH NEW YORK, Abraham Cahan. Film Hester Street based on Yekl (1896). Novel, other stories among first about Jewish immigrants on N.Y.'s East Side. 240pp. 5⅜ x 8½. 22427-9 Pa. $6.95

SELECTED POEMS, Walt Whitman. Generous sampling from *Leaves of Grass.* Twenty-four poems include "I Hear America Singing," "Song of the Open Road," "I Sing the Body Electric," "When Lilacs Last in the Dooryard Bloom'd," "O Captain! My Captain!"—all reprinted from an authoritative edition. Lists of titles and first lines. 128pp. 5³⁄₁₆ x 8¼. 26878-0 Pa. $1.00

THE BEST TALES OF HOFFMANN, E. T. A. Hoffmann. 10 of Hoffmann's most important stories: "Nutcracker and the King of Mice," "The Golden Flowerpot," etc. 458pp. 5⅜ x 8½. 21793-0 Pa. $9.95

FROM FETISH TO GOD IN ANCIENT EGYPT, E. A. Wallis Budge. Rich detailed survey of Egyptian conception of "God" and gods, magic, cult of animals, Osiris, more. Also, superb English translations of hymns and legends. 240 illustrations. 545pp. 5⅜ x 8½. 25803-3 Pa. $13.95

FRENCH STORIES/CONTES FRANÇAIS: A Dual-Language Book, Wallace Fowlie. Ten stories by French masters, Voltaire to Camus: "Micromegas" by Voltaire; "The Atheist's Mass" by Balzac; "Minuet" by de Maupassant; "The Guest" by Camus, six more. Excellent English translations on facing pages. Also French-English vocabulary list, exercises, more. 352pp. 5⅜ x 8½. 26443-2 Pa. $8.95

CHICAGO AT THE TURN OF THE CENTURY IN PHOTOGRAPHS: 122 Historic Views from the Collections of the Chicago Historical Society, Larry A. Viskochil. Rare large-format prints offer detailed views of City Hall, State Street, the Loop, Hull House, Union Station, many other landmarks, circa 1904-1913. Introduction. Captions. Maps. 144pp. 9⅜ x 12¼. 24656-6 Pa. $12.95

OLD BROOKLYN IN EARLY PHOTOGRAPHS, 1865-1929, William Lee Younger. Luna Park, Gravesend race track, construction of Grand Army Plaza, moving of Hotel Brighton, etc. 157 previously unpublished photographs. 165pp. 8⅞ x 11¾. 23587-4 Pa. $13.95

THE MYTHS OF THE NORTH AMERICAN INDIANS, Lewis Spence. Rich anthology of the myths and legends of the Algonquins, Iroquois, Pawnees and Sioux, prefaced by an extensive historical and ethnological commentary. 36 illustrations. 480pp. 5⅜ x 8½. 25967-6 Pa. $8.95

AN ENCYCLOPEDIA OF BATTLES: Accounts of Over 1,560 Battles from 1479 B.C. to the Present, David Eggenberger. Essential details of every major battle in recorded history from the first battle of Megiddo in 1479 B.C. to Grenada in 1984. List of Battle Maps. New Appendix covering the years 1967-1984. Index. 99 illustrations. 544pp. 6½ x 9¼. 24913-1 Pa. $14.95

SAILING ALONE AROUND THE WORLD, Captain Joshua Slocum. First man to sail around the world, alone, in small boat. One of great feats of seamanship told in delightful manner. 67 illustrations. 294pp. 5⅜ x 8½. 20326-3 Pa. $5.95

ANARCHISM AND OTHER ESSAYS, Emma Goldman. Powerful, penetrating, prophetic essays on direct action, role of minorities, prison reform, puritan hypocrisy, violence, etc. 271pp. 5⅜ x 8½. 22484-8 Pa. $6.95

MYTHS OF THE HINDUS AND BUDDHISTS, Ananda K. Coomaraswamy and Sister Nivedita. Great stories of the epics; deeds of Krishna, Shiva, taken from puranas, Vedas, folk tales; etc. 32 illustrations. 400pp. 5⅜ x 8½. 21759-0 Pa. $10.95

BEYOND PSYCHOLOGY, Otto Rank. Fear of death, desire of immortality, nature of sexuality, social organization, creativity, according to Rankian system. 291pp. 5⅜ x 8½. 20485-5 Pa. $8.95

A THEOLOGICO-POLITICAL TREATISE, Benedict Spinoza. Also contains unfinished Political Treatise. Great classic on religious liberty, theory of government on common consent. R. Elwes translation. Total of 421pp. 5⅜ x 8½. 20249-6 Pa. $9.95

MY BONDAGE AND MY FREEDOM, Frederick Douglass. Born a slave, Douglass became outspoken force in antislavery movement. The best of Douglass' autobiographies. Graphic description of slave life. 464pp. 5⅜ x 8½. 22457-0 Pa. $8.95

FOLLOWING THE EQUATOR: A Journey Around the World, Mark Twain. Fascinating humorous account of 1897 voyage to Hawaii, Australia, India, New Zealand, etc. Ironic, bemused reports on peoples, customs, climate, flora and fauna, politics, much more. 197 illustrations. 720pp. 5⅜ x 8½. 26113-1 Pa. $15.95

THE PEOPLE CALLED SHAKERS, Edward D. Andrews. Definitive study of Shakers: origins, beliefs, practices, dances, social organization, furniture and crafts, etc. 33 illustrations. 351pp. 5⅜ x 8½. 21081-2 Pa. $8.95

THE MYTHS OF GREECE AND ROME, H. A. Guerber. A classic of mythology, generously illustrated, long prized for its simple, graphic, accurate retelling of the principal myths of Greece and Rome, and for its commentary on their origins and significance. With 64 illustrations by Michelangelo, Raphael, Titian, Rubens, Canova, Bernini and others. 480pp. 5⅜ x 8½. 27584-1 Pa. $9.95

PSYCHOLOGY OF MUSIC, Carl E. Seashore. Classic work discusses music as a medium from psychological viewpoint. Clear treatment of physical acoustics, auditory apparatus, sound perception, development of musical skills, nature of musical feeling, host of other topics. 88 figures. 408pp. 5⅜ x 8½. 21851-1 Pa. $10.95

THE PHILOSOPHY OF HISTORY, Georg W. Hegel. Great classic of Western thought develops concept that history is not chance but rational process, the evolution of freedom. 457pp. 5⅜ x 8½. 20112-0 Pa. $9.95

THE BOOK OF TEA, Kakuzo Okakura. Minor classic of the Orient: entertaining, charming explanation, interpretation of traditional Japanese culture in terms of tea ceremony. 94pp. 5⅜ x 8½. 20070-1 Pa. $3.95

LIFE IN ANCIENT EGYPT, Adolf Erman. Fullest, most thorough, detailed older account with much not in more recent books, domestic life, religion, magic, medicine, commerce, much more. Many illustrations reproduce tomb paintings, carvings, hieroglyphs, etc. 597pp. 5⅜ x 8½. 22632-8 Pa. $11.95

SUNDIALS, Their Theory and Construction, Albert Waugh. Far and away the best, most thorough coverage of ideas, mathematics concerned, types, construction, adjusting anywhere. Simple, nontechnical treatment allows even children to build several of these dials. Over 100 illustrations. 230pp. 5⅜ x 8½. 22947-5 Pa. $7.95

DYNAMICS OF FLUIDS IN POROUS MEDIA, Jacob Bear. For advanced students of ground water hydrology, soil mechanics and physics, drainage and irrigation engineering, and more. 335 illustrations. Exercises, with answers. 784pp. 6⅛ x 9¼. 65675-6 Pa. $19.95

SONGS OF EXPERIENCE: Facsimile Reproduction with 26 Plates in Full Color, William Blake. 26 full-color plates from a rare 1826 edition. Includes "TheTyger," "London," "Holy Thursday," and other poems. Printed text of poems. 48pp. 5¼ x 7. 24636-1 Pa. $4.95

OLD-TIME VIGNETTES IN FULL COLOR, Carol Belanger Grafton (ed.). Over 390 charming, often sentimental illustrations, selected from archives of Victorian graphics—pretty women posing, children playing, food, flowers, kittens and puppies, smiling cherubs, birds and butterflies, much more. All copyright-free. 48pp. 9¼ x 12¼. 27269-9 Pa. $7.95

PERSPECTIVE FOR ARTISTS, Rex Vicat Cole. Depth, perspective of sky and sea, shadows, much more, not usually covered. 391 diagrams, 81 reproductions of drawings and paintings. 279pp. 5⅜ x 8½. 22487-2 Pa. $7.95

DRAWING THE LIVING FIGURE, Joseph Sheppard. Innovative approach to artistic anatomy focuses on specifics of surface anatomy, rather than muscles and bones. Over 170 drawings of live models in front, back and side views, and in widely varying poses. Accompanying diagrams. 177 illustrations. Introduction. Index. 144pp. 8⅜ x11¼. 26723-7 Pa. $8.95

GOTHIC AND OLD ENGLISH ALPHABETS: 100 Complete Fonts, Dan X. Solo. Add power, elegance to posters, signs, other graphics with 100 stunning copyright-free alphabets: Blackstone, Dolbey, Germania, 97 more–including many lower-case, numerals, punctuation marks. 104pp. 8⅛ x 11. 24695-7 Pa. $8.95

HOW TO DO BEADWORK, Mary White. Fundamental book on craft from simple projects to five-bead chains and woven works. 106 illustrations. 142pp. 5⅜ x 8. 20697-1 Pa. $4.95

THE BOOK OF WOOD CARVING, Charles Marshall Sayers. Finest book for beginners discusses fundamentals and offers 34 designs. "Absolutely first rate . . . well thought out and well executed."–E. J. Tangerman. 118pp. 7¾ x 10⅝. 23654-4 Pa. $6.95

ILLUSTRATED CATALOG OF CIVIL WAR MILITARY GOODS: Union Army Weapons, Insignia, Uniform Accessories, and Other Equipment, Schuyler, Hartley, and Graham. Rare, profusely illustrated 1846 catalog includes Union Army uniform and dress regulations, arms and ammunition, coats, insignia, flags, swords, rifles, etc. 226 illustrations. 160pp. 9 x 12. 24939-5 Pa. $10.95

WOMEN'S FASHIONS OF THE EARLY 1900s: An Unabridged Republication of "New York Fashions, 1909," National Cloak & Suit Co. Rare catalog of mail-order fashions documents women's and children's clothing styles shortly after the turn of the century. Captions offer full descriptions, prices. Invaluable resource for fashion, costume historians. Approximately 725 illustrations. 128pp. 8⅜ x 11¼. 27276-1 Pa. $11.95

THE 1912 AND 1915 GUSTAV STICKLEY FURNITURE CATALOGS, Gustav Stickley. With over 200 detailed illustrations and descriptions, these two catalogs are essential reading and reference materials and identification guides for Stickley furniture. Captions cite materials, dimensions and prices. 112pp. 6½ x 9¼. 26676-1 Pa. $9.95

EARLY AMERICAN LOCOMOTIVES, John H. White, Jr. Finest locomotive engravings from early 19th century: historical (1804–74), main-line (after 1870), special, foreign, etc. 147 plates. 142pp. 11⅜ x 8¼. 22772-3 Pa. $10.95

THE TALL SHIPS OF TODAY IN PHOTOGRAPHS, Frank O. Braynard. Lavishly illustrated tribute to nearly 100 majestic contemporary sailing vessels: Amerigo Vespucci, Clearwater, Constitution, Eagle, Mayflower, Sea Cloud, Victory, many more. Authoritative captions provide statistics, background on each ship. 190 black-and-white photographs and illustrations. Introduction. 128pp. 8⅞ x 11¾. 27163-3 Pa. $13.95

EARLY NINETEENTH-CENTURY CRAFTS AND TRADES, Peter Stockham (ed.). Extremely rare 1807 volume describes to youngsters the crafts and trades of the day: brickmaker, weaver, dressmaker, bookbinder, ropemaker, saddler, many more. Quaint prose, charming illustrations for each craft. 20 black-and-white line illustrations. 192pp. 4⅝ x 6. 27293-1 Pa. $4.95

VICTORIAN FASHIONS AND COSTUMES FROM HARPER'S BAZAR, 1867–1898, Stella Blum (ed.). Day costumes, evening wear, sports clothes, shoes, hats, other accessories in over 1,000 detailed engravings. 320pp. 9⅜ x 12¼. 22990-4 Pa. $14.95

GUSTAV STICKLEY, THE CRAFTSMAN, Mary Ann Smith. Superb study surveys broad scope of Stickley's achievement, especially in architecture. Design philosophy, rise and fall of the Craftsman empire, descriptions and floor plans for many Craftsman houses, more. 86 black-and-white halftones. 31 line illustrations. Introduction 208pp. 6½ x 9¼. 27210-9 Pa. $9.95

THE LONG ISLAND RAIL ROAD IN EARLY PHOTOGRAPHS, Ron Ziel. Over 220 rare photos, informative text document origin (1844) and development of rail service on Long Island. Vintage views of early trains, locomotives, stations, passengers, crews, much more. Captions. 8⅞ x 11¾. 26301-0 Pa. $13.95

THE BOOK OF OLD SHIPS: From Egyptian Galleys to Clipper Ships, Henry B. Culver. Superb, authoritative history of sailing vessels, with 80 magnificent line illustrations. Galley, bark, caravel, longship, whaler, many more. Detailed, informative text on each vessel by noted naval historian. Introduction. 256pp. 5⅜ x 8½. 27332-6 Pa. $7.95

TEN BOOKS ON ARCHITECTURE, Vitruvius. The most important book ever written on architecture. Early Roman aesthetics, technology, classical orders, site selection, all other aspects. Morgan translation. 331pp. 5⅜ x 8½. 20645-9 Pa. $8.95

THE HUMAN FIGURE IN MOTION, Eadweard Muybridge. More than 4,500 stopped-action photos, in action series, showing undraped men, women, children jumping, lying down, throwing, sitting, wrestling, carrying, etc. 390pp. 7⅞ x 10⅝. 20204-6 Clothbd. $25.95

TREES OF THE EASTERN AND CENTRAL UNITED STATES AND CANADA, William M. Harlow. Best one-volume guide to 140 trees. Full descriptions, woodlore, range, etc. Over 600 illustrations. Handy size. 288pp. 4½ x 6⅜. 20395-6 Pa. $6.95

SONGS OF WESTERN BIRDS, Dr. Donald J. Borror. Complete song and call repertoire of 60 western species, including flycatchers, juncoes, cactus wrens, many more–includes fully illustrated booklet. Cassette and manual 99913-0 $8.95

GROWING AND USING HERBS AND SPICES, Milo Miloradovich. Versatile handbook provides all the information needed for cultivation and use of all the herbs and spices available in North America. 4 illustrations. Index. Glossary. 236pp. 5⅜ x 8½. 25058-X Pa. $6.95

BIG BOOK OF MAZES AND LABYRINTHS, Walter Shepherd. 50 mazes and labyrinths in all–classical, solid, ripple, and more–in one great volume. Perfect inexpensive puzzler for clever youngsters. Full solutions. 112pp. 8⅛ x 11. 22951-3 Pa. $4.95

PIANO TUNING, J. Cree Fischer. Clearest, best book for beginner, amateur. Simple repairs, raising dropped notes, tuning by easy method of flattened fifths. No previous skills needed. 4 illustrations. 201pp. 5⅜ x 8½. 23267-0 Pa. $6.95

A SOURCE BOOK IN THEATRICAL HISTORY, A. M. Nagler. Contemporary observers on acting, directing, make-up, costuming, stage props, machinery, scene design, from Ancient Greece to Chekhov. 611pp. 5⅜ x 8½. 20515-0 Pa. $12.95

THE COMPLETE NONSENSE OF EDWARD LEAR, Edward Lear. All nonsense limericks, zany alphabets, Owl and Pussycat, songs, nonsense botany, etc., illustrated by Lear. Total of 320pp. 5⅜ x 8½. (USO) 20167-8 Pa. $6.95

VICTORIAN PARLOUR POETRY: An Annotated Anthology, Michael R. Turner. 117 gems by Longfellow, Tennyson, Browning, many lesser-known poets. "The Village Blacksmith," "Curfew Must Not Ring Tonight," "Only a Baby Small," dozens more, often difficult to find elsewhere. Index of poets, titles, first lines. xxiii + 325pp. 5⅝ x 8¼. 27044-0 Pa. $8.95

DUBLINERS, James Joyce. Fifteen stories offer vivid, tightly focused observations of the lives of Dublin's poorer classes. At least one, "The Dead," is considered a masterpiece. Reprinted complete and unabridged from standard edition. 160pp. 5$\frac{3}{16}$ x 8¼. 26870-5 Pa. $1.00

THE HAUNTED MONASTERY and THE CHINESE MAZE MURDERS, Robert van Gulik. Two full novels by van Gulik, set in 7th-century China, continue adventures of Judge Dee and his companions. An evil Taoist monastery, seemingly supernatural events; overgrown topiary maze hides strange crimes. 27 illustrations. 328pp. 5⅜ x 8½. 23502-5 Pa. $8.95

THE BOOK OF THE SACRED MAGIC OF ABRAMELIN THE MAGE, translated by S. MacGregor Mathers. Medieval manuscript of ceremonial magic. Basic document in Aleister Crowley, Golden Dawn groups. 268pp. 5⅜ x 8½. 23211-5 Pa. $8.95

NEW RUSSIAN-ENGLISH AND ENGLISH-RUSSIAN DICTIONARY, M. A. O'Brien. This is a remarkably handy Russian dictionary, containing a surprising amount of information, including over 70,000 entries. 366pp. 4½ x 6⅛. 20208-9 Pa. $9.95

HISTORIC HOMES OF THE AMERICAN PRESIDENTS, Second, Revised Edition, Irvin Haas. A traveler's guide to American Presidential homes, most open to the public, depicting and describing homes occupied by every American President from George Washington to George Bush. With visiting hours, admission charges, travel routes. 175 photographs. Index. 160pp. 8¼ x 11. 26751-2 Pa. $11.95

NEW YORK IN THE FORTIES, Andreas Feininger. 162 brilliant photographs by the well-known photographer, formerly with *Life* magazine. Commuters, shoppers, Times Square at night, much else from city at its peak. Captions by John von Hartz. 181pp. 9¼ x 10¾. 23585-8 Pa. $12.95

INDIAN SIGN LANGUAGE, William Tomkins. Over 525 signs developed by Sioux and other tribes. Written instructions and diagrams. Also 290 pictographs. 111pp. 6⅛ x 9¼. 22029-X Pa. $3.95

CATALOG OF DOVER BOOKS

ANATOMY: A Complete Guide for Artists, Joseph Sheppard. A master of figure drawing shows artists how to render human anatomy convincingly. Over 460 illustrations. 224pp. 8⅜ x 11¼. 27279-6 Pa. $10.95

MEDIEVAL CALLIGRAPHY: Its History and Technique, Marc Drogin. Spirited history, comprehensive instruction manual covers 13 styles (ca. 4th century thru 15th). Excellent photographs; directions for duplicating medieval techniques with modern tools. 224pp. 8⅜ x 11¼. 26142-5 Pa. $12.95

DRIED FLOWERS: How to Prepare Them, Sarah Whitlock and Martha Rankin. Complete instructions on how to use silica gel, meal and borax, perlite aggregate, sand and borax, glycerine and water to create attractive permanent flower arrangements. 12 illustrations. 32pp. 5⅜ x 8½. 21802-3 Pa. $1.00

EASY-TO-MAKE BIRD FEEDERS FOR WOODWORKERS, Scott D. Campbell. Detailed, simple-to-use guide for designing, constructing, caring for and using feeders. Text, illustrations for 12 classic and contemporary designs. 96pp. 5⅜ x 8½. 25847-5 Pa. $2.95

SCOTTISH WONDER TALES FROM MYTH AND LEGEND, Donald A. Mackenzie. 16 lively tales tell of giants rumbling down mountainsides, of a magic wand that turns stone pillars into warriors, of gods and goddesses, evil hags, powerful forces and more. 240pp. 5⅜ x 8½. 29677-6 Pa. $6.95

THE HISTORY OF UNDERCLOTHES, C. Willett Cunnington and Phyllis Cunnington. Fascinating, well-documented survey covering six centuries of English undergarments, enhanced with over 100 illustrations: 12th-century laced-up bodice, footed long drawers (1795), 19th-century bustles, 19th-century corsets for men, Victorian "bust improvers," much more. 272pp. 5⅝ x 8¼. 27124-2 Pa. $9.95

ARTS AND CRAFTS FURNITURE: The Complete Brooks Catalog of 1912, Brooks Manufacturing Co. Photos and detailed descriptions of more than 150 now very collectible furniture designs from the Arts and Crafts movement depict davenports, settees, buffets, desks, tables, chairs, bedsteads, dressers and more, all built of solid, quarter-sawed oak. Invaluable for students and enthusiasts of antiques, Americana and the decorative arts. 80pp. 6½ x 9¼. 27471-3 Pa. $8.95

HOW WE INVENTED THE AIRPLANE: An Illustrated History, Orville Wright. Fascinating firsthand account covers early experiments, construction of planes and motors, first flights, much more. Introduction and commentary by Fred C. Kelly. 76 photographs. 96pp. 8¼ x 11. 25662-6 Pa. $8.95

THE ARTS OF THE SAILOR: Knotting, Splicing and Ropework, Hervey Garrett Smith. Indispensable shipboard reference covers tools, basic knots and useful hitches; handsewing and canvas work, more. Over 100 illustrations. Delightful reading for sea lovers. 256pp. 5⅜ x 8½. 26440-8 Pa. $7.95

FRANK LLOYD WRIGHT'S FALLINGWATER: The House and Its History, Second, Revised Edition, Donald Hoffmann. A total revision–both in text and illustrations–of the standard document on Fallingwater, the boldest, most personal architectural statement of Wright's mature years, updated with valuable new material from the recently opened Frank Lloyd Wright Archives. "Fascinating"–*The New York Times*. 116 illustrations. 128pp. 9¼ x 10¾. 27430-6 Pa. $11.95

PHOTOGRAPHIC SKETCHBOOK OF THE CIVIL WAR, Alexander Gardner. 100 photos taken on field during the Civil War. Famous shots of Manassas Harper's Ferry, Lincoln, Richmond, slave pens, etc. 244pp. 10⅝ x 8¼. 22731-6 Pa. $9.95

FIVE ACRES AND INDEPENDENCE, Maurice G. Kains. Great back-to-the-land classic explains basics of self-sufficient farming. The one book to get. 95 illustrations. 397pp. 5⅜ x 8½. 20974-1 Pa. $7.95

SONGS OF EASTERN BIRDS, Dr. Donald J. Borror. Songs and calls of 60 species most common to eastern U.S.: warblers, woodpeckers, flycatchers, thrushes, larks, many more in high-quality recording. Cassette and manual 99912-2 $9.95

A MODERN HERBAL, Margaret Grieve. Much the fullest, most exact, most useful compilation of herbal material. Gigantic alphabetical encyclopedia, from aconite to zedoary, gives botanical information, medical properties, folklore, economic uses, much else. Indispensable to serious reader. 161 illustrations. 888pp. 6½ x 9¼. 2-vol. set. (USO) Vol. I: 22798-7 Pa. $9.95
Vol. II: 22799-5 Pa. $9.95

HIDDEN TREASURE MAZE BOOK, Dave Phillips. Solve 34 challenging mazes accompanied by heroic tales of adventure. Evil dragons, people-eating plants, blood-thirsty giants, many more dangerous adversaries lurk at every twist and turn. 34 mazes, stories, solutions. 48pp. 8¼ x 11. 24566-7 Pa. $2.95

LETTERS OF W. A. MOZART, Wolfgang A. Mozart. Remarkable letters show bawdy wit, humor, imagination, musical insights, contemporary musical world; includes some letters from Leopold Mozart. 276pp. 5⅜ x 8½. 22859-2 Pa. $7.95

BASIC PRINCIPLES OF CLASSICAL BALLET, Agrippina Vaganova. Great Russian theoretician, teacher explains methods for teaching classical ballet. 118 illustrations. 175pp. 5⅜ x 8½. 22036-2 Pa. $5.95

THE JUMPING FROG, Mark Twain. Revenge edition. The original story of The Celebrated Jumping Frog of Calaveras County, a hapless French translation, and Twain's hilarious "retranslation" from the French. 12 illustrations. 66pp. 5⅜ x 8½. 22686-7 Pa. $3.95

BEST REMEMBERED POEMS, Martin Gardner (ed.). The 126 poems in this superb collection of 19th- and 20th-century British and American verse range from Shelley's "To a Skylark" to the impassioned "Renascence" of Edna St. Vincent Millay and to Edward Lear's whimsical "The Owl and the Pussycat." 224pp. 5⅜ x 8½. 27165-X Pa. $4.95

COMPLETE SONNETS, William Shakespeare. Over 150 exquisite poems deal with love, friendship, the tyranny of time, beauty's evanescence, death and other themes in language of remarkable power, precision and beauty. Glossary of archaic terms. 80pp. 5³⁄₁₆ x 8¼. 26686-9 Pa. $1.00

BODIES IN A BOOKSHOP, R. T. Campbell. Challenging mystery of blackmail and murder with ingenious plot and superbly drawn characters. In the best tradition of British suspense fiction. 192pp. 5⅜ x 8½. 24720-1 Pa. $6.95

THE WIT AND HUMOR OF OSCAR WILDE, Alvin Redman (ed.). More than 1,000 ripostes, paradoxes, wisecracks: Work is the curse of the drinking classes; I can resist everything except temptation; etc. 258pp. 5⅜ x 8½.   20602-5 Pa. $5.95

SHAKESPEARE LEXICON AND QUOTATION DICTIONARY, Alexander Schmidt. Full definitions, locations, shades of meaning in every word in plays and poems. More than 50,000 exact quotations. 1,485pp. 6½ x 9¼. 2-vol. set.
Vol. 1: 22726-X Pa. $16.95
Vol. 2: 22727-8 Pa. $16.95

SELECTED POEMS, Emily Dickinson. Over 100 best-known, best-loved poems by one of America's foremost poets, reprinted from authoritative early editions. No comparable edition at this price. Index of first lines. 64pp. 5³⁄₁₆ x 8¼.
26466-1 Pa. $1.00

CELEBRATED CASES OF JUDGE DEE (DEE GOONG AN), translated by Robert van Gulik. Authentic 18th-century Chinese detective novel; Dee and associates solve three interlocked cases. Led to van Gulik's own stories with same characters. Extensive introduction. 9 illustrations. 237pp. 5⅜ x 8½.   23337-5 Pa. $6.95

THE MALLEUS MALEFICARUM OF KRAMER AND SPRENGER, translated by Montague Summers. Full text of most important witchhunter's "bible," used by both Catholics and Protestants. 278pp. 6⅝ x 10.   22802-9 Pa. $12.95

SPANISH STORIES/CUENTOS ESPAÑOLES: A Dual-Language Book, Angel Flores (ed.). Unique format offers 13 great stories in Spanish by Cervantes, Borges, others. Faithful English translations on facing pages. 352pp. 5⅜ x 8½.
25399-6 Pa. $8.95

THE CHICAGO WORLD'S FAIR OF 1893: A Photographic Record, Stanley Appelbaum (ed.). 128 rare photos show 200 buildings, Beaux-Arts architecture, Midway, original Ferris Wheel, Edison's kinetoscope, more. Architectural emphasis; full text. 116pp. 8¼ x 11.   23990-X Pa. $9.95

OLD QUEENS, N.Y., IN EARLY PHOTOGRAPHS, Vincent F. Seyfried and William Asadorian. Over 160 rare photographs of Maspeth, Jamaica, Jackson Heights, and other areas. Vintage views of DeWitt Clinton mansion, 1939 World's Fair and more. Captions. 192pp. 8⅞ x 11.   26358-4 Pa. $12.95

CAPTURED BY THE INDIANS: 15 Firsthand Accounts, 1750-1870, Frederick Drimmer. Astounding true historical accounts of grisly torture, bloody conflicts, relentless pursuits, miraculous escapes and more, by people who lived to tell the tale. 384pp. 5⅜ x 8½.   24901-8 Pa. $8.95

THE WORLD'S GREAT SPEECHES, Lewis Copeland and Lawrence W. Lamm (eds.). Vast collection of 278 speeches of Greeks to 1970. Powerful and effective models; unique look at history. 842pp. 5⅜ x 8½.   20468-5 Pa. $14.95

THE BOOK OF THE SWORD, Sir Richard F. Burton. Great Victorian scholar/adventurer's eloquent, erudite history of the "queen of weapons"–from prehistory to early Roman Empire. Evolution and development of early swords, variations (sabre, broadsword, cutlass, scimitar, etc.), much more. 336pp. 6⅛ x 9¼.
25434-8 Pa. $9.95

AUTOBIOGRAPHY: The Story of My Experiments with Truth, Mohandas K. Gandhi. Boyhood, legal studies, purification, the growth of the Satyagraha (nonviolent protest) movement. Critical, inspiring work of the man responsible for the freedom of India. 480pp. 5⅜ x 8½. (USO) 24593-4 Pa. $8.95

CELTIC MYTHS AND LEGENDS, T. W. Rolleston. Masterful retelling of Irish and Welsh stories and tales. Cuchulain, King Arthur, Deirdre, the Grail, many more. First paperback edition. 58 full-page illustrations. 512pp. 5⅜ x 8½. 26507-2 Pa. $9.95

THE PRINCIPLES OF PSYCHOLOGY, William James. Famous long course complete, unabridged. Stream of thought, time perception, memory, experimental methods; great work decades ahead of its time. 94 figures. 1,391pp. 5⅜ x 8½. 2-vol. set.
Vol. I: 20381-6 Pa. $12.95
Vol. II: 20382-4 Pa. $12.95

THE WORLD AS WILL AND REPRESENTATION, Arthur Schopenhauer. Definitive English translation of Schopenhauer's life work, correcting more than 1,000 errors, omissions in earlier translations. Translated by E. F. J. Payne. Total of 1,269pp. 5⅜ x 8½. 2-vol. set. Vol. 1: 21761-2 Pa. $11.95
Vol. 2: 21762-0 Pa. $12.95

MAGIC AND MYSTERY IN TIBET, Madame Alexandra David-Neel. Experiences among lamas, magicians, sages, sorcerers, Bonpa wizards. A true psychic discovery. 32 illustrations. 321pp. 5⅜ x 8½. (USO) 22682-4 Pa. $8.95

THE EGYPTIAN BOOK OF THE DEAD, E. A. Wallis Budge. Complete reproduction of Ani's papyrus, finest ever found. Full hieroglyphic text, interlinear transliteration, word-for-word translation, smooth translation. 533pp. 6½ x 9¼.
21866-X Pa. $10.95

MATHEMATICS FOR THE NONMATHEMATICIAN, Morris Kline. Detailed, college-level treatment of mathematics in cultural and historical context, with numerous exercises. Recommended Reading Lists. Tables. Numerous figures. 641pp. 5⅜ x 8½.
24823-2 Pa. $11.95

THEORY OF WING SECTIONS: Including a Summary of Airfoil Data, Ira H. Abbott and A. E. von Doenhoff. Concise compilation of subsonic aerodynamic characteristics of NACA wing sections, plus description of theory. 350pp. of tables. 693pp. 5⅜ x 8½. 60586-8 Pa. $14.95

THE RIME OF THE ANCIENT MARINER, Gustave Doré, S. T. Coleridge. Doré's finest work; 34 plates capture moods, subtleties of poem. Flawless full-size reproductions printed on facing pages with authoritative text of poem. "Beautiful. Simply beautiful."–*Publisher's Weekly.* 77pp. 9¼ x 12. 22305-1 Pa. $6.95

NORTH AMERICAN INDIAN DESIGNS FOR ARTISTS AND CRAFTSPEOPLE, Eva Wilson. Over 360 authentic copyright-free designs adapted from Navajo blankets, Hopi pottery, Sioux buffalo hides, more. Geometrics, symbolic figures, plant and animal motifs, etc. 128pp. 8⅜ x 11. (EUK) 25341-4 Pa. $8.95

SCULPTURE: Principles and Practice, Louis Slobodkin. Step-by-step approach to clay, plaster, metals, stone; classical and modern. 253 drawings, photos. 255pp. 8⅛ x 11.
22960-2 Pa. $11.95

THE INFLUENCE OF SEA POWER UPON HISTORY, 1660–1783, A. T. Mahan. Influential classic of naval history and tactics still used as text in war colleges. First paperback edition. 4 maps. 24 battle plans. 640pp. 5⅜ x 8½. 25509-3 Pa. $12.95

THE STORY OF THE TITANIC AS TOLD BY ITS SURVIVORS, Jack Winocour (ed.). What it was really like. Panic, despair, shocking inefficiency, and a little heroism. More thrilling than any fictional account. 26 illustrations. 320pp. 5⅜ x 8½.
20610-6 Pa. $8.95

FAIRY AND FOLK TALES OF THE IRISH PEASANTRY, William Butler Yeats (ed.). Treasury of 64 tales from the twilight world of Celtic myth and legend: "The Soul Cages," "The Kildare Pooka," "King O'Toole and his Goose," many more. Introduction and Notes by W. B. Yeats. 352pp. 5⅜ x 8½. 26941-8 Pa. $8.95

BUDDHIST MAHAYANA TEXTS, E. B. Cowell and Others (eds.). Superb, accurate translations of basic documents in Mahayana Buddhism, highly important in history of religions. The Buddha-karita of Asvaghosha, Larger Sukhavativyuha, more. 448pp. 5⅜ x 8½. 25552-2 Pa. $12.95

ONE TWO THREE . . . INFINITY: Facts and Speculations of Science, George Gamow. Great physicist's fascinating, readable overview of contemporary science: number theory, relativity, fourth dimension, entropy, genes, atomic structure, much more. 128 illustrations. Index. 352pp. 5⅜ x 8½. 25664-2 Pa. $8.95

ENGINEERING IN HISTORY, Richard Shelton Kirby, et al. Broad, nontechnical survey of history's major technological advances: birth of Greek science, industrial revolution, electricity and applied science, 20th-century automation, much more. 181 illustrations. ". . . excellent . . ."–*Isis.* Bibliography. vii + 530pp. 5⅜ x 8¼.
26412-2 Pa. $14.95

DALÍ ON MODERN ART: The Cuckolds of Antiquated Modern Art, Salvador Dalí. Influential painter skewers modern art and its practitioners. Outrageous evaluations of Picasso, Cézanne, Turner, more. 15 renderings of paintings discussed. 44 calligraphic decorations by Dalí. 96pp. 5⅜ x 8½. (USO) 29220-7 Pa. $4.95

ANTIQUE PLAYING CARDS: A Pictorial History, Henry René D'Allemagne. Over 900 elaborate, decorative images from rare playing cards (14th–20th centuries): Bacchus, death, dancing dogs, hunting scenes, royal coats of arms, players cheating, much more. 96pp. 9¼ x 12¼. 29265-7 Pa. $11.95

MAKING FURNITURE MASTERPIECES: 30 Projects with Measured Drawings, Franklin H. Gottshall. Step-by-step instructions, illustrations for constructing handsome, useful pieces, among them a Sheraton desk, Chippendale chair, Spanish desk, Queen Anne table and a William and Mary dressing mirror. 224pp. 8⅛ x 11¼.
29338-6 Pa. $13.95

THE FOSSIL BOOK: A Record of Prehistoric Life, Patricia V. Rich et al. Profusely illustrated definitive guide covers everything from single-celled organisms and dinosaurs to birds and mammals and the interplay between climate and man. Over 1,500 illustrations. 760pp. 7½ x 10⅛. 29371-8 Pa. $29.95

Prices subject to change without notice.

Available at your book dealer or write for free catalog to Dept. GI, Dover Publications, Inc., 31 East 2nd St., Mineola, N.Y. 11501. Dover publishes more than 500 books each year on science, elementary and advanced mathematics, biology, music, art, literary history, social sciences and other areas.